13763

Env. 47

G is for ecoGarden

is for ecoGarden

An A – Z Guide to an
Organically Healthy Garden

Nigel Dudley and Sue Stickland

Gaia Books Limited

A GAIA ORIGINAL

Conceived by Joss Pearson

Editorial Gian Douglas Home, Fiona Trent

Design Marnie Searchwell

Illustration Babz Scott (The Garden Studio)

Direction Jonathan Hilton, Patrick Nugent

Consultants Dr Jeremy Light (Biological Coordinator at the Centre for Alternative Technology, Wales)
Dr Andrew Watterson (Lecturer in Industrial and Health Studies at Southampton University)

® This is a Registered Trade Mark of Gaia Books Limited.

First published in the United Kingdom in 1991 by
Gaia Books Limited
66 Charlotte Street
London, WIP ILR

Printed and bound in Italy by Rotolito s.p.a. on enviromentally friendly paper, with less than 0.5 kilos of chlorine per 100 kilos of paper.

British Library Cataloguing in Publication Data
Dudley, Nigel
  G is for (eco)Garden.
  1. Gardening
  I. Title II. Stickland, Sue
  635.0484

  ISBN 1-85675-035-3

10 9 8 7 6 5 4 3 2 1

Most of us have gardens of some sort, and enjoy looking after them. Yet how many of us have a true understanding of the intricate system of plant and animal relationships on which the health of the garden ecosystem depends? Figures show that, on average, as much as one *kilo* of active ingredient is sprayed or poured on to every acre of domestic garden annually. This chemical onslaught not only destroys the pests, diseases, and weeds on which it is targetted, but does untold damage to the soil, water, and air, and to the myriad beneficial organisms, from microbes to mammals, with which you share the garden.

This book advocates a harmonious system of gardening – working with nature and without chemicals. In adopting it, you will be making a significant contribution to restoring balance in your part of the natural world. Get to know your garden so that you can position your plants where they are most likely to thrive. Assist the natural cycles of death, decay, and regeneration by using a compost heap. Introduce diversity: a garden pond or mixed hedge will attract a variety of species. Put the plants that encourage the natural enemies of garden pests to work for you.

How to use this book

Entries are arranged alphabetically. Ingredient names, used on an increasing number of commercial products, are listed instead of brand names, which tend to vary. Within entries, **bold** words cross-refer you to supplementary information, as well as to safe, natural alternatives to chemicals. There are entries on a wide range of garden plants, the pests and diseases that commonly afflict them, and the natural-gardening products and techniques used to nurture them. Illustrated features introduce different eco-designs, and there is a comprehensive listing of suppliers and organizations at the back.

Writing this book has been an exciting experiment in cooperation between the Henry Doubleday Research Association and the Soil Association (respectively, Britain's leading authorities on organic gardening and organic farming). We hope that the combination of experience has produced a thought-provoking guide that will be of use to gardeners everywhere.

Nigel Dudley and Sue Stickland
Bristol and Ryton-on-Dunsmore, June 1991

Acaricide any **pesticide** used against **spiders** and mites, including **red spider mites**. In addition to killing harmless spiders, acaricides can damage other **beneficial insects** and cause a range of health and environmental effects.

Acid rain a secondary effect of **air pollution**. Chemical reactions between sulphur dioxide or nitrogen oxides and moisture in the atmosphere create the sulphuric and nitric acid that falls as acid rain. This pollutes freshwaters, killing fish and other aquatic life, and also damages **trees**. **Vegetable** and **fruit** crops and, possibly, other flowering plants may also be affected. See **Energy** for ways in which you can help to reduce acid rain.

Acid soil a **soil** with a **pH** below 7.0, generally indicating a low **lime** content. Most plants, particularly **vegetables**, grow well on slightly acid soils. However, in very acid conditions (with a pH level below 5.0), **phosphorus**, one of the main plant **nutrients**, becomes "locked up" in the soil and unavailable to plants, and other **minerals** may be washed out. **Earthworms** and the soil **microorganisms**, which break down **organic matter**, cannot tolerate excessively acid conditions (with a pH below 4.5). Correct over-acidity by adding lime to the soil.

Aerobic bacterial decomposition a type of bacterial decomposition carried out in the presence of oxygen. This should be the main process in a **compost heap** and is essential if you are to make good **compost**. To help ensure that the heap remains aerobic, keep it well aerated by including some fibrous material, such as **straw**. The best way to aerate a garden heap is to turn it over with a fork. See also **Anaerobic bacterial decomposition**.

Aerosol any dispersed substance expelled from a **spray** can by a propellant under pressure. Aerosol sprays are often used to apply **pesticides** to house plants, and many fly and **mosquito** sprays also come in this form. Aerosols containing chlorofluorocarbon propellants (**CFCs**) contribute to the depletion of the **ozone** layer. Most of those on sale today contain other safer propellants. Ideally, avoid spraying, or use alternative devices, such as the pump-action spray. If you do buy aerosols, ensure that they are marked "CFC free". Never spray near food or young children.

   Several pesticides that are suspected **carcinogens**, such as artificial **pyrethroids**, are available as aerosols. These are particularly dangerous because they can be easily inhaled.

Agrochemical any artificial chemical used in farming or gardening, including **pesticides** and many **fertilizers**, feed additives, and veterinary products. Many agrochemicals cause damage to the environment during manufacture and use and when disposed of. For example, some of the **nitrate leaching** into oceans comes from fertilizer factories, which also consume huge amounts of **energy** in the form of fossil fuels. **Persistent** pesticides remain hazardous to the environment long after they have been used or leaked from factories, while the burning of unwanted agrochemicals can cause significant and hazardous **air pollution**. See also **Pesticides** and **Fertilizers, artificial**.

Air pollution any form of pollution that depletes air quality. In urban and suburban areas, high concentrations of air pollutants, such as sulphur dioxide, nitrogen oxides, **ozone**, and hydrocarbons, may be present in gardens. Such concentrations may be harmful to the overall health of the garden ecosystem, but little is yet known about their effects on individual plants. Some scientists now believe that high pollution levels in rural areas may be responsible for reducing crop yields by as much as 5%. If you are gardening in a polluted environment, particularly close to a busy road where airborne **lead** may be a problem, wash homegrown **fruit** and **vegetables** with extra care. However, even this may not remove all trace of pollutants since some may be systemic, being taken up and remaining within the body of a plant.

Alfalfa a deep-rooting, perennial **green manure**, *Medicago sativa*. It is a **legume**, and will fix **nitrogen** if the necessary **bacteria** are present in the **soil**. Cut the foliage down two or three times a year (see **Green manures** chart, pp. 80-1) and use it on the **compost heap** or as a **mulch**. You can also use alfalfa seeds for **sprouting**.

Alkaline soil a **soil** with a **pH** above 7.0, generally indicating a high **lime** content. If the soil becomes too alkaline (with a pH level above 7.5), some plant **nutrients**, in particular **trace elements**, become "locked up" in the soil and unavailable to plants. Correcting over-alkalinity is not easy, but working in **organic matter** will help.

Allelopath any plant that releases toxic chemicals into the **soil** from its roots, preventing other plants from growing nearby and reducing competition as a result. The rhododendron is a good example of an allelopath, and you will rarely find other plants growing near or underneath it.

Allergen any substance that is capable of causing an allergic reaction, in which the body becomes hypersensitive to the substance in question. Common allergens that you may encounter in a garden include pollen and a whole range of artificial chemicals and materials. Many garden **pesticides** are allergens.

A small number of people show natural sensitivity to one or more allergens, while others may become sensitized following prolonged exposure to an **irritant**. Allergic reactions are frequently difficult to diagnose because they often resemble the common cold, with sore eyes and throat, and a runny nose.

If you are a hay-fever sufferer or have a tendency to allergic reactions, you should take extra care not to be caught in pesticide **spray drift**.

Allethrin an **insecticide** of the **pyrethroid** group. It can cause contact **dermatitis**, and is a suspected **mutagen**. Allethrin is harmful to **bees** and fish. Try **cultural control, biological control, barriers**, and **traps** instead. Only resort to the use of **natural insecticides**, such as **derris**, if all else fails.

Allotment in the UK, a small area of land owned by a local authority, which you can rent cheaply for growing **vegetables** and **flowers**. In renting an allotment, you have certain obligations to keep it in good order and under productive cultivation. In some areas, allotments are in high demand and there may be long waiting lists; many allotments are also under threat from developers. Allotments are usually grouped together and thus are a good way to meet other gardeners and learn about the best crops to grow in your particular area.

Alloxydim sodium a **translocated herbicide** used for couch grass control around **root crops, peas, strawberries**, and **shrubs**. It is a potential eye and skin **irritant** with a **harvest interval** of four to eight weeks. Alloxydim sodium is likely to remain **persistent** in the **soil** for several weeks. Although couch grass is a tough **weed**, you can remove it effectively on a garden scale by applying a **mulch** or forking regularly (see **Weed control** chart, pp. 182-3).

Alum another name for **Aluminium sulphate**.

Aluminium ammonium sulphate an inorganic animal repellent, sprayed on to **vegetables, fruit** trees, and ornamentals to protect against **bird** and animal **pests**. You should not use it in **organic gardening**, where acceptable alternatives include bird **netting, fencing** against **rabbits**, and the use of a cat to deter **mice** and **rats**.

Aluminium sulphate a **molluscicide** used against **slugs**. It has a reputation for being one of the safer chemical treatments, but is both poisonous and an eye and skin **irritant**. See **Slugs** for safer, alternative methods of control.

Aminotriazole a **translocated herbicide** used, either alone or in mixtures with **simazine** or **2,4-D**, for **weed control** on uncultivated land. It is slightly irritating to the eyes and skin and there is some indication that it may be a **carcinogen**: the Swedish government banned it following evidence that railway workers using aminotriazole showed higher than average rates of tumours. It has also been identified as a possible **mutagen** and a potent anti-thyroid agent. Amino-triazole can cause damage to nearby plants through **spray drift**. In addition to Sweden, Norway and Finland have either banned or severely restricted it, and its use on food crops is no longer allowed in the USA. Use safer options for **clearing ground**, such as **mulches**.

Amitrole another name for **Aminotriazole**.

Ammonium sulphamate a **translocated**, **soil**-acting **herbicide** used for general **weed control**, including **trees**, on uncultivated land. It is a potential skin, eye, respiratory, and gastro-intestinal **irritant**, and can cause extensive damage to other plants through **spray drift** and because of its **persistence** in the soil: **trees** may suffer if their roots extend into recently treated soil. Use safer alternatives for **clearing ground**, such as **mulches**.

Anaerobic bacterial decomposition a type of bacterial decomposition that takes place in the absence of oxygen. Anaerobic **bacteria** usually give off **methane** as a by-product. You should prevent anaerobic conditions predominating in your **compost heap**, otherwise instead of sweet-smelling, friable **compost**, you will produce a slimy, foul-smelling mess. By following the principles of good compost-making and ensuring that enough oxygen gets into the heap, you can avoid this risk. See also **Aerobic bacterial decomposition**.

Anthocorid bugs small black or brown **beneficial insects** (see p. 16), about 4mm ($\frac{1}{6}$in) in length, which are important **natural predators** of **fruit** and **vegetable pests**. Their diet includes **aphids**, **root aphids**, **capsid bugs**, **caterpillars**, **red spider mites**, and **scale insects**.

Anticholinesterase any of a group of chemicals that interferes with the transmission of messages to the nerves. A minority of people are very susceptible to anticholinesterase compounds and can suffer trembling, dizziness, weakness, or even collapse after relatively mild contamination. Commercially available anticholinesterase products, which include many **carbamate** and **organophosphorus pesticides**, usually carry warnings so that people who know they are at risk can avoid them.

Ant killers a range of different chemical **insecticides**, used to kill **ants** and usually sold in powder or granule form; many ant killers contain highly dangerous chemicals, such as **gamma HCH**. Ants do little harm in a garden so there is no reason to harm them. If you encourage **hedgehogs** and some insectivorous **birds**, such as tits, these will feed on ants and help to keep them under control.

Ants small insects that lead a communal lifestyle. Ants are usually fairly harmless in the garden, although they can sometimes damage bulbs and seedlings. Encourage their **natural predators**, for example **hedgehogs** and insectivorous **birds**, to help keep numbers under control. Commercially available chemical **ant killers** are frequently highly toxic and unacceptable in an organic garden.

Ant killers
Ants
Aphids

Aphids small, soft-bodied insects, which are common **pests** in the garden; there may be winged and wingless forms in any colony. Aphids are often simply called "greenfly" or "blackfly", although there are in fact many different types of varying colours. They feed on plant sap, which weakens the plants and distorts their growth. They also secrete a sticky "honeydew" on which black sooty moulds may grow. This can spoil the appearance of a plant and its fruit, and reduce the amount of light reaching the leaves. Aphids can also transmit **virus** diseases.

Some aphids will attack only a single, or a small number of, plant species; others are wider ranging. They are more likely to attack plants that are under stress, or those that have made over-lush growth. Thus, the first preventative measure you can take is to ensure that your plants have good growing conditions and a balanced food supply. You can also encourage the aphids' many natural enemies, which include **hoverflies**, **ladybirds**, and **lacewings**. There is a specific **biological control**, a predatory midge called *Aphidoletes*, for controlling aphids in **greenhouses**. *Aphidoletes* is also used on some outdoor crops.

Look out for early signs of attack since you may be able to prevent the damage spreading by picking off infested leaves or shoots. As a last resort, spray with **insecticidal soap**. With low-growing **vegetable** crops, you can use a covering of **fleece** as a sure way of preventing an attack, especially if there is a risk of **virus** infection being spread by the aphids. See also **Root aphids** and **Woolly aphid**.

11

Apple an adaptable **fruit tree**, which will grow in a wider range of conditions than most. You can grow apple trees on dwarfing **rootstocks** or train them against **walls** or **fencing**, so that there is always room for one or more specimens, even in a small garden. They look attractive both in flower and fruit, and by choosing the right **varieties** you can be eating your own apples for much of the autumn and winter. Although apple trees crop best on a sunny, sheltered site in deep, fertile **soil**, some varieties are more tolerant than others. A variety widely grown in your area and suited to local conditions is often more likely to succeed than a popular commercial one. On a poor soil or with a weak variety, it is advisable to choose a more vigorous rootstock.

An apple tree will not give a good crop unless **pollination** takes place with a different variety. Thus, check the pollination group of trees before buying them. **Aphids**, **apple sawfly**, **codling moth**, **woolly aphid**, and **winter moth** are the main apple **pests**. The most troublesome **diseases** are powdery **mildew**, **apple scab**, **apple and pear canker**, and **brown rot**, but look out for less susceptible varieties.

Apple and pear canker a common **disease** of **apples**, **pears**, and some other trees, such as **hawthorn**. It causes sunken wounds in bark and, in extreme cases, girdled branches may die. Fruit may develop a brown rot around the eye.

Trees planted on heavy, badly drained **soils** are more prone to canker. Reduce the likelihood of the disease by planting less susceptible **varieties**. Ensure that **drainage** is good, and also that trees are not overfed. Prune out and burn any cankered branches as soon as you see them.

Apple sawfly see **Sawfly**.

Apple scab a common **disease** of **apples**. The first symptoms show as greenish brown blotches on the leaves, which later turn to black. Dark spots then appear on the fruit, developing into cork-textured scabs, and blisters form on the twigs. Reduce the likelihood of scab by planting less susceptible varieties. To break the cycle of infection, rake up and remove fallen leaves; alternatively, encourage them to decompose by running a rotary mower over them or spraying them with a **liquid feed**. Prune out infected twigs in winter.

12

Artichoke, globe a perennial **vegetable**, which is decorative enough to grow in a **flower** border if you have no room in your **vegetable** plot. Harvest the edible flowerheads while still tightly closed, but try to leave a few to open for the **bees**. Globe artichokes like a sunny, sheltered spot and a well-drained **soil**, rich in **organic matter**. **Aphids** are likely to be the only serious **pest**.

Artichoke, Jerusalem an easy-to-grow **vegetable**, which produces knobbly, edible tubers. You get the best crop if you replant the tubers in a different plot each spring and add **organic matter** to the **soil**. Jerusalem artichokes are not closely related to other vegetables, and will fit anywhere within a crop **rotation**. However, try to dig up all old tubers or they will regrow and become **weeds**. Jerusalem artichokes can reach up to 3m (9ft) tall, so you can use them as protective **windbreaks**.

Asbestos a highly dangerous, fibrous, heat-resistant, substance, formerly used as a building material in garden sheds. It is one of the most carcinogenic substances known and is capable of causing a range of serious and fatal conditions, including lung cancer and asbestosis. All types of asbestos are hazardous to health, but to varying extents. Some, but not all, types have been banned in the UK, but you may well come across old asbestos when demolishing or restoring old buildings. Treat it with caution and do not inhale particles. If you have, or suspect you have, asbestos in your home or garden, contact your local authority for professional advice as to whether it should be removed or left untouched. *Do not attempt to remove it yourself.*

Ash, common a **tree**, *Fraxinus excelsior*, native to Britain, which you can plant as a specimen or as part of a **hedge**. **Coppicing** it will encourage it to grow strong, straight poles, which make excellent **tool** handles. Ash trees are declining in some areas of Britain. The cause has not yet been established but one theory is that the use of **fungicides** destroys certain beneficial **fungi** associated with the ash and weakens the tree as a result.

Asparagus a perennial **vegetable**, regarded as a luxury crop because it takes up a lot of space and only has a short cropping season. It is traditionally grown on **raised beds**, but in light **soil** you can plant it on the flat. Alternatively, cut the edible young shoots from plants grown for their ferny foliage in a **flower**bed. Asparagus needs good **drainage** and plenty of sunshine. **Slugs** and **asparagus beetle** are the most troublesome **pests**.

Asparagus beetle a conspicuous yellow and black chequered **beetle**, up to 6mm (¹/₄in) long, which is a damaging **pest** of **asparagus**. The adult beetles and their grey or black larvae feed on the leaves and stems in summer and can do severe damage. Reduce their numbers by clearing up any plant debris in winter, since this is where many adults will hibernate. If the beetles reappear in spring, spray with **derris** as a last resort.

Asters hardy perennial plants with daisy-like flowers. There are many different species of aster. Those with single flowerheads are good **attractant plants** and are also popular with **bees** and **butterflies**, flowering late into the autumn. There are dwarf and tall varieties, with flowers mainly in shades of mauve and pink. Asters grow best on a sunny site in well-drained but moisture-retentive **soil**. Many asters are prone to powdery **mildew**, although some species, such as *Aster* x *frikartii*, are less susceptible.

Astrological planting see **Biodynamic gardening**.

Asulam a **translocated herbicide** of the **carbamate** group, used for dock control on established grassland, and around some types of **fruit tree**. Although it is one of the less toxic carbamates, **spray drift** can cause damage and application near young grass and trees can check growth. You can control docks in the garden by applying a **mulch**, or **digging** to remove the roots (see **Weed control** chart, pp. 182-3).

Atrazine a soil-acting **herbicide**, employed as a selective weedkiller on some crops but used for general **weed control** in gardens, particularly on **paths**. It is an eye, skin, and respiratory system **irritant** and, when heated, may release poisonous gases. The UN International Labour Organization lists it as having moderate cumulative toxicity. There is some evidence that atrazine may be a **mutagen** and, in 1989, the US Environmental Protection Agency listed it as being **oncogenic** and possibly a **carcinogen**. It is **persistent**, and detectable in the **soil** for at least seven months after use. Atrazine is highly toxic to aquatic life, even at quite low concentrations, and since maximum permissible concentrations in water are regularly exceeded in many parts of the European Community, use of this chemical is likely to be restricted in future. Try hand **weeding**, **hoeing**, forking, or apply a **mulch** instead.

Attractant plants plants that encourage the **natural predators** and **parasites** of garden **pests**. **Beneficial insects**, such as **hoverflies**, **lacewings**, and **ichneumon flies**, usually prefer single, flat, open **flowers** from which they can easily extract nectar and/or pollen. Good attractant plants are single **asters**, **Californian poppies**, annual **convolvulus**, **goldenrod**, **nasturtium**, **poached-egg plant**, **buckwheat**, **phacelia**, **yarrow**, and many **umbellifers**, such as **sea holly**, fennel, and dill.

Some simple "cottage garden" plants, for example, cornflowers and hollyhocks, are also effective, but avoid highly bred, double **varieties**. Those that flower very early or late in the season are particularly useful because they provide food for insects preparing for, or emerging from, hibernation. Other plants, for instance **pyracantha** and **cotoneaster**, have berries or seeds which will attract potential pest-eating **birds**. **Ground cover plants** provide shelter for a range of natural predators, including **ground beetles**.

Aubergine a half-hardy plant, grown for its deep purple fruit. In a cool climate, aubergines are best planted in a **greenhouse** or under a **cloche**. In any crop **rotation**, keep them in a plot with **tomatoes**. Their main **pests** are **aphids** and **red spider mites**.

1 Ladybird
2 Ladybird larva
3 Hoverfly
4 Hoverfly larva
5 Anthocorid bug
6 Lacewing
7 Ground beetle
8 Centipede

Beneficial insects

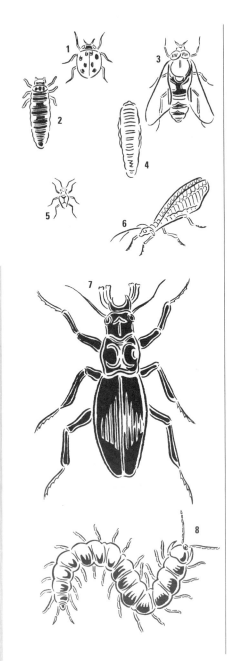

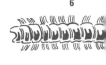

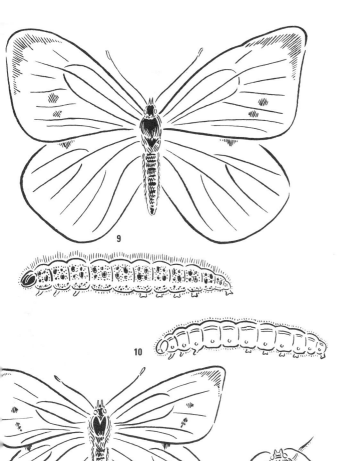

1 Capsid bug
2 Cutworm
3 Wireworm
4 Click beetle
5 Gooseberry
  sawfly larva
6 Millipede
7 Mealybug
8 Scale insect
9 Large white
  butterfly and
  caterpillar
10 Small white
  butterfly and
  caterpillar
11 Cabbage
  moth and
  caterpillar

All insects are shown approximately twice actual size

Insect pests

Bacillus thuringiensis (BT) a naturally occurring **bacterium**, which kills certain types of **caterpillar**. It is commercially available as a **spray**, which you can use as a form of **biological control** against some **cabbage caterpillars** – those of the large and small white butterfly and the cabbage moth. Spray the leaves of infested **brassica** plants with BT. Only when a caterpillar has eaten sprayed leaves will the bacteria become active within its gut. Thus, BT cannot harm other insects, and is unlikely to reach the wrong caterpillars; it is not **persistent**.

Bacteria a large group of **microorganisms**, usually classified as plants. Most garden bacteria are beneficial, playing key roles in the breakdown of plant and animal material. They are active in the creation of **compost**, the release of **natural fertilizers**, and the maintenance of a healthy **humus** layer in the **soil**. **Symbiotic** bacteria, present in some soils, form nodules on the roots of **legumes** and fix **nitrogen** from the air, thus helping to maintain **nutrient** levels. Some types of bacteria are **parasites**, causing a range of plant **diseases**, including **halo blight**.

Bark, shredded a useful **mulch** for **shrubs** and perennial **flower**beds, and as a surface layer on **paths**. It is slow to break down and therefore good for **weed control**. Do not dig it into the **soil** since it can cause depletion of **nitrogen**. Instead, allow it to be gradually taken under by **earthworms**

and it will add **organic matter** and **nutrients** to the soil. Fresh coniferous bark contains resins which inhibit plant growth, so leave any you purchase or collect to weather before use. Finely shredded bark breaks down quite quickly; it is useful in small quantities in **potting composts**.

Barrier any physical structure that helps to protect your plants from **pests**. Ordinary garden **netting** keeps off **birds**, cats, and dogs, while a smaller, 1cm-square mesh works against the large and the small white **butterfly**. Very fine materials or **fleeces** will keep out small pests such as **fleabeetles**, **aphids**, **carrot flies**, and **cabbage root flies**. You can also make cabbage-root-fly barriers by fitting squares of **carpet** underlay closely around stems at ground level. Use homemade **bottle cloches** to protect young plants from **slugs**, or sharp barriers, such as a ring of crushed **egg shells**. Be sure to put any barrier in place before the pest arrives, otherwise you may actually make the problem worse by trapping it inside.

Bat a harmless mammal that eats many flying insect **pests**. Bat numbers have declined catastrophically throughout the industrialized world due to **habitat** destruction, poisoning by **agrochemicals**, and the use of **wood preservatives** that are also **pesticides**, such as **gamma HCH** (also known as lindane) and **pentachlorphenol**. For treating roof timber, avoid use of wood preservatives, or choose those that do not harm bats, such as **permethrin** (see also **Timber treatment**). If you have bats in your roof, shed, or barn, you are bound by law to inform your local English Nature office or the equivalent body in your area (see Useful Addresses, pp. 190-1). They will let you have a list of bat-friendly wood preservatives on request. Bats do no harm and you can attract them into your garden by building a bat box. This should be not less than 12 x 15cm (5 x 6in) by 10cm (4in) deep, with a rectangular entrance slit on the underside, 4 x 1.5cm ($1^3/_4$ x $^3/_4$in). Use untreated wood because the bats will cling to the roof of the box by their feet. Do not expect immediate results – a box usually has to be in place for a few years before bats will adopt it.

Beans summer **vegetables**, grown for their pods and/or seeds; the commonest types are French, runner, and broad beans. They are **legumes** and can fix **nitrogen** in the

soil if the necessary **bacteria** are present. Grow them with **peas** in your crop **rotation** and use a demanding crop, such as **brassicas**, to succeed them the following year to take advantage of the nitrogen.

Broad beans are very hardy and will give an early summer crop. Eat the young pods whole, or leave them to mature and shell them; the shoot tips are also edible. All other beans are half hardy. Climbing French and runner beans need supporting on a framework of canes or strings, but give good yields over a long period, and can look very attractive. French beans set better than runners in hot weather. Dwarf French beans are useful for a quick crop, particularly if grown under **cloches** at the beginning and end of the season. As well as eating the young green beans, you can dry the seeds for use as haricots.

All beans need a soil rich in **organic matter**. French beans do best on a sunny, sheltered site, whereas runners tolerate light shade. **Slugs** and **blackfly** are common **pests** of all beans. Broad beans are also affected by **chocolate spot** and **pea and bean weevil**. French and runner beans suffer from **halo blight**, but look out for **resistant varieties**.

Bed system
Bees

Bed system a system of growing **vegetables** in which the garden is divided up into beds, 1.2–1.4m (5ft) wide, separated by narrow **paths**; also known as the intensive bed system. Such a design enables you to do all the planting, **weeding**, and harvesting without treading on the beds, so there is no risk of damage to the **soil structure**. Plant the beds closely since you will not need to walk between the plants and, in general, use equidistant **plant spacing**. The beds will give a high yield, even when the area taken up by the paths is taken into account, and the closely spaced crops prevent **weed** growth.

The beds tend to become raised because you are cultivating them and adding **organic matter**, and yet treading down the surrounding paths. This can help **drainage** and enable you to make an earlier start in spring.

You can incorporate **organic matter** or **green manures** into the beds by **digging**. However, you usually need to dig less on a bed system because there is no **compaction** of the soil, and many people do not dig them at all.

Bees major pollinators of **flowers** and **vegetables**. You can attract bees by planting highly aromatic plants, or those with single, open, colourful flowers, containing plenty of nectar and/or pollen. Plants in the Labiatae family, which includes many **herbs**, are good for bees. Avoid highly bred, double-flower forms because bees find it difficult reach their nectar.

Beekeeping for honey is possible on quite a small scale, but honey bees need a lot of attention and someone on hand to catch them when they swarm. They do not usually sting unless frightened or attacked.

Bees are badly affected by the use of **pesticides** and many colonies are destroyed every year. If you keep bees in the country, contact a local beekeeping group: they may be able to let you know when farmers are spraying so that you can keep hives closed. See also **Pollination**.

Beetles a large group of insects, most species of which are fairly harmless, although a few will eat leaves, bulbs, or flowerheads. **Ground beetles** are **beneficial insects** which you should encourage since they help to control **slugs**.

Beetroot see **Root crops**.

Bendiocarb a **contact** and **systemic insecticide** of the **carbamate** group, used against a range of **pests** on **beans**, **courgettes**, and **squashes**. Bendiocarb is poisonous, an **anti-cholinesterase** compound, and a skin **irritant**. It is dangerous to fish and **birds** and toxic to **bees**. Try **cultural control**, **biological control**, **barriers**, and **traps** instead. Only resort to **natural insecticides**, such as **derris**, if all else fails.

Beneficial insects various insects that are useful in the garden because they prey on **pests**. They include **anthocorid bugs**, **centipedes**, **ground beetles**, **hoverflies**, **lacewings**, and **ladybirds**. It is important to recognize both the adults and the larvae of these helpful creatures (see p. 16) so that you do not kill them in error, and also so that you can encourage them in the garden.

First and foremost, stop using **insecticides** that will harm them. Use even **natural insecticides** with caution because they too can kill beneficial insects. Next, take steps to supply them with suitable sources of food by growing **attractant plants** and make sure that there are plenty of places for them to shelter in and hibernate: nooks and crannies in old logs or **walls**, or dense climbing plants, for example. In return, these beneficial creatures will play a significant role in reducing pest numbers.

Benomyl a **systemic fungicide** used to treat **fungi**, including moulds and some **leaf spots**. It is a mild skin **irritant** and has been identified, together with its **metabolite carbendazim**, as a potential **carcinogen**, **teratogen**, and **mutagen**. Finland has banned it because of feared genetic risks, and in Sweden garden use of benomyl is illegal. Although it is not particularly toxic to **bees**, research has shown that it can harm **earthworms** and other **soil** life when used around **fruit trees**, and there is a growing number of pathogens that show **resistance** to benomyl. Try **cultural control** instead.

Berberis any spiny shrub of the genus *Berberis* with yellow or orange flowers, which are loved by **bees**. There are many species, both dwarf and tall, deciduous and evergreen. All grow well in most garden **soils**, either in sun or partial shade. You can plant them in a border or as an informal and impenetrable **hedge**. Those varieties that bear berries will attract **birds**.

Benomyl
Berberis
Big bud
Bioallethrin
Biodegradable

Big bud a condition affecting **blackcurrants**, caused by **gall** mites. These infest the buds, which become swollen and fail to develop. Affected buds are easiest to spot in winter and early spring, when you should remove and destroy them to kill the enclosed mites. The mites may also carry **blackcurrant reversion**, a common viral **disease**.

Bioallethrin an **insecticide** of the **pyrethroid** group, only available in mixtures, usually with **permethrin**. At present, there is very little information available on this chemical. See also **Permethrin**.

Biodegradable describing any organically derived material that can be broken down into its constituent parts through the activity of **bacteria** or other natural biological processes. In theory, you can use anything that is biodegradable as a source of **nutrients** in the garden. In practice, however, gardeners are usually only interested in things which break down fairly quickly, such as plant debris, **household scraps** including **kitchen waste**, and **manure**, and they often speed up the decomposition process by adding these materials to a garden **compost heap**.

Biodynamic gardening a specialized variation of **organic gardening**, invented by the German philosopher Rudolf Steiner, and now widely practised in mainland Europe. Biodynamic gardeners time the sowing and planting of particular groups of plants by the cycles of the moon and stars; harvesting of different parts of a plant is also governed by these factors. You can purchase annual biodynamic charts to help you work out your gardening calendar for the year. Biodynamic gardeners also use special "preparations" to stimulate plant growth and other biological processes. Most organic certification schemes accept food produced by biodynamic methods.

Biological control the use of one creature or organism to control another. You are applying this general principle when, for example, you encourage **natural predators** and **parasites** into your garden by growing **attractant plants**. However, you can also introduce specific biological controls. Two of the most successful are for **greenhouse pests**: the predatory mite, ***Phytoseiulus persimilis***, feeds on the **red spider mite**, and a **parasitic wasp**, *Encarsia formosa*, is effective against glasshouse **whitefly**. There is also a greenhouse control for **mealybug**. You can order these controls from mail-order suppliers (see Useful Addresses, pp. 190-1). Other greenhouse biological controls, such as one for **vine weevil**, have been used by commercial growers for some time and are now becoming available to gardeners.

In the garden, it is more difficult to use introduced predators or parasites effectively since you cannot so easily control conditions, and there is no guarantee that the creatures will stay. However, some preparations of **bacteria** or **fungi** as control agents are effective. The bacterium *Bacillus thuringiensis* kills a range of **butterfly** and moth **caterpillars**, and a preparation of the fungus *Trichoderma viride* has been used as a control against **silver leaf disease**.

There are strict regulations controlling which organisms can be brought in for biological control. But as long as they have been shown to kill only their target, they can be a safe and effective method of **pest and disease control**. Follow carefully any instructions for use and storage accompanying a biological control.

Bioresmethrin a **contact insecticide** of the **pyrethroid** group, used against a wide range of **pests**. It has low mammalian toxicity and appears to have few detrimental health effects on humans. However, it is extremely toxic to insects, including **beneficial insects** and **bees**. Try **cultural control**, **biological control**, **barriers**, and **traps** instead. Only resort to **natural insecticides**, such as **derris**, if all else fails.

Birds both **natural predators** and **pests** in the garden. A healthy population of birds can help control insect pests, including **slugs** and **snails**, although some species, such as blackbirds, thrushes, and starlings, also feed on beneficial **earthworms**. Do all you can to encourage a range of bird species in your garden by supplying a **bird table** from which to feed them during the winter, by planting **flowers** and **shrubs** with seedheads and berries, and by providing **nest boxes** and dense foliage cover.

Birds eat seeds and, occasionally, **fruit** and some flowers, so you may need to protect vulnerable plants with some form of **barrier** or **birdscarer**. Bush and **cane fruit** are particular favourites and are best planted in a **fruit cage**.

Birdscarers devices designed to scare off marauding **birds**. These include: glittering strips of foil, hung on lines or attached to canes; commercially available humming line or old video or cassette tape, which you can string across crops and which will make a noise in the wind; toy windmills; and, of course, scarecrows. Birds soon get used to these devices so, in order for them to be effective, move or change them every week or so. See also **Netting**.

Bird table usually a simple construction, consisting of a flat surface with a lipped edge on which **birds** can perch, fixed to a straight pole with some support at the base. The lipped edge also helps to prevent food falling off. Place your bird table well out of reach of cats and other predators, for example, not directly under an overhanging branch. Suitable food for attracting a variety of species includes nuts, grains, meat scraps, fat, coconut shells, seeds, and breadcrumbs. For small, agile birds, such as tits (which are also timid), you can suspend a netted bag of peanuts or half an upside-down coconut from the base of the table, where only they can reach it. Avoid stodgy food, particularly sodden lumps of bread, which are lacking in nutrients and can expand inside birds' stomachs, causing harm to young ones. Feed the birds mainly in

Birds
Birdscarers
Bird table

winter so that, in summer months, they will concentrate on eating garden **pests**. Your bird table will also be visited by far more species in winter.

Bitterpit a disorder of **apples** caused by **calcium** deficiency and indicated by dark spots, both on the skin surface and scattered throughout the flesh. Bitterpit may mean that calcium is deficient in the **soil**, or that it unavailable to the **trees** for some reason. Check the **pH** of the soil and, if it is low, apply **lime** or **dolomite** to bring it to 6.5. Ensure that the trees have adequate moisture, and do not overfeed them since excess **nitrogen** and **potassium** can cause calcium to become "locked-up" in the soil.

Bitumen a black, impermeable substance, resembling tar, which is used on roofs, **paths**, and the outsides of garden sheds to prevent water penetrating. Bitumen is a poison, a skin **irritant**, and a **carcinogen**. Do not to breathe in fumes while using it and always wear **protective clothing**.

Bitterpit
Bitumen
Blackberries
Blackcurrant reversion
Blackcurrants
Blackfly
Black kneed capsid
Blackspot

Blackberries see **Cane fruit**.

Blackcurrant reversion a common viral **disease** of **blackcurrants**, which causes poor flowering and greatly reduced yields. It is usually spread by the **gall** mites that cause **big bud**, or by propagation from infected bushes. Always buy stock from a reputable source. Lift out and burn infected bushes in winter before buying new ones.

Blackcurrants see **Bush fruit**.

Blackfly see **Aphids**.

Black kneed capsid see **Capsid bugs**.

Blackspot a widespread fungal **disease** affecting most types of rose. It is indicated by dark brown or black spots on the leaves, which may drop, and weakened growth. The disease is more likely to occur and also more likely to be severe in warm, wet conditions. Reduce the likelihood of blackspot by growing less susceptible **varieties** and by ensuring that plants are not overshadowed or too closely crowded together. Remove any infected leaves during summer, where practical to do so. Disease spores overwinter on leaves and shoots, so you can reduce the chances of reinfection by collecting fallen leaves in autumn (or by laying a **mulch** over the top of them), and by **pruning** hard in spring.

Blight see **Potato and tomato blight**.

Blood a source of **nitrogen**, purchasable in its dried form for use as a **natural fertilizer** or as an addition to the **compost heap**. It is, however, unsuitable for use in **organic gardening** because it acts too quickly, and is, of course, unacceptable to vegetarians or anyone practising **vegan gardening**.

Blossom end rot a disorder of **tomatoes**, in which a rounded, dark brown patch forms at one end of the fruit and gradually hardens. It is caused by a lack of **calcium** in the fruit tissue. This does not usually mean that there is a deficiency in the **soil**, only that calcium has not moved up through the plant. A humid atmosphere or lack of water at the roots are common reasons for this disorder, since either can prevent water and hence calcium from moving up the plant. You should therefore ensure that ventilation is good and not allow plants to dry out.

Bone meal ground-up bones sold for use as a **natural fertilizer**. Bone meal is a good source of slowly released **phosphorus**, and also contains some **nitrogen** and **calcium**. Use it when planting **fruit**, roses, and **shrubs** on poor **soils** or when **soil testing** shows that phosphorus levels are low. It may also benefit **vegetable** crops. Finely ground bone meal and bone flour release their **nutrients** more quickly than coarsely ground forms, and are therefore more suitable for short-term crops. Always buy bone meal that has been steam sterilized because in its raw form it can carry the disease anthrax. Bone meal is unacceptable in **vegan gardening**, and other sources of phosphorus, such as the **rock fertilizer**, rock phosphate, must be used.

Bonfire a traditional method of disposing of woody plant debris, but one not recommended for regular use in **organic gardening**. Not only do bonfires destroy many valuable **nutrients** that would be better returned to the **soil**, they also present a serious health risk. Wood smoke, especially that released from slow-burning fires, is highly carcinogenic. It contains roughly the same mix of **carcinogens** as cigarette smoke, but in far higher concentrations. It can also cause severe smarting of the eyes as well as sore throats and coughs. Large bonfires release gases that contribute to **global warming**.

You can put most plant debris, except woody or diseased material, straight on to the **compost heap**. Store small woody branches outside where they will break down in time: nooks and crannies in the pile will also provide a home for insects. Alternatively, you can invest in a garden **shredder** that converts woody branches into a useful **mulch** or **compost** material. As a last resort, send material to the local dump, or burn it in the home, ideally when it is dry. If you do light the occasional bonfire, avoid doing so in the early morning or evening when the smoke is likely to hang around, or when it is windy.

Bootlace fungus see **Honey fungus**.

Borax an **insecticide** widely used against **ants**; its technical name is sodium tetraborate. Borax is also employed as a **wood preservative** and is recommended by English Nature (see Useful Addresses, pp. 190-1) as being relatively safe for **bats**. However, it is poisonous, a skin **irritant**, and there is some evidence linking boric acid compounds, such as borax, to reduced fertility following long exposure. There is no reason to harm ants in the garden, although you can encourage **hedgehogs** and insectivorous **birds** to help keep numbers down.

Bordeaux mixture a **copper fungicide** made out of a mixture of **copper sulphate** and hydrated **lime**. It is one of the safer **fungicides** accepted in **organic gardening**, although in the UK, members of the Soil Association (see Useful Addresses, pp. 190-1) symbol scheme are only permitted to use it in some instances, for example, when growing **vines** for wine. Bordeaux mixture is one of the less toxic and environmentally damaging **pesticides** available, but it would be wrong to assume that it is completely safe since there is evidence that its principle ingredient, copper sulphate, is **oncogenic** and a **mutagen**. Copper is **persistent** in the **soil** and can harm some plants. Continual application of Bordeaux mixture can reduce **potato** yields. Only use it as a last resort when **cultural control** has failed.

Bootlace fungus

Borax

Bordeaux mixture

Botrytis a common fungal **disease** which causes rots in a wide range of **flower**, **fruit**, and **vegetable** crops. It is indicated by a fluffy, grey mould, which may have black bodies scattered in it. Botrytis is a serious problem on **strawberries** and **lettuce**, particularly in **greenhouses**, and it affects the flowers of chrysanthemums and other plants. To help prevent the disease, ensure that plants are not overcrowded, and avoid overhead watering. In greenhouses, increase ventilation and temperature. Good **hygiene** is vital since the fungus will grow on any dead tissue.

Bottle cloche a glass or plastic bottle with the bottom cut off, which you can use as a type of **cloche** for covering and protecting individual young plants. Bottle cloches create a warm atmosphere for the plants and also protect them against **pests**, especially **slugs**. However, you need to be careful not to trap the pests inside. You can remove the tops of the bottles to provide ventilation.

Bracken a fern, *Pteridium aquilinum*, and a source of nutrients and organic matter. There is some evidence that the spores and/or exudates from the roots or stems are **carcinogens**. The compounds implicated are believed to decompose readily into harmless substances when added to the **compost heap** or when mixed with normal to **alkaline soils**. It is safer to compost bracken than use it as a **mulch**. In **acid soils**, exudates may remain harmful longer. Although richest in **nutrients** when green, bracken is likely to contain higher concentrations of toxins at this stage in its growth. Beware of collecting bracken in late summer when there is a risk of inhaling spores.

  If you want to clear bracken off your ground, cut it two or three times a year for three years, ideally by breaking off the young shoots with a stick just after they have sprouted. Bracken has a dense network of rhizomes beneath the soil, but, once cut, it is worth **digging** over ground in August to expose the roots. Wait two years before planting recently cleared land with **vegetables** or other food crops. Remove bracken from the catchment area of any well used for drinking water.

Brandling worms small red worms, used to carry out the composting process that takes place in **wormbins**. You can collect them from piles of **manure** or leaves in which they live, or buy them from a fishing shop in season, since they are used as bait.

Brassicas plants of the cabbage family, which includes a large number of our common **vegetables**: brussels sprouts, kale, cauliflower, calabrese, broccoli, swedes, and turnips, as well as the many types of cabbage. You should grow all these on the same plot in your crop **rotation**, and **lime** it if necessary to prevent a build-up of **clubroot disease**.

Leafy brassicas, in particular, like a fairly rich **soil**, so you may need to add some **compost** or well-rotted **manure**. Alternatively, organize your rotation scheme so that they come after **nitrogen**-fixing **legumes** and an overwintering **green manure** crop of **grazing rye**.

By growing a range of brassicas, you can have fresh vegetables almost all year round. As well as cabbages, kale, and broccoli for winter use, a number of hardy oriental brassicas, such as pak choi and Japanese mustards, will produce leaves for winter salads, especially if you have a **greenhouse** or **cloches**.

Unfortunately, all brassicas suffer from a number of common **pests** and diseases. Young plants usually need protection from **slugs** and **cabbage root fly**. Clubroot is the most troublesome disease, but look out for reported **resistant varieties** of swede and calabrese. Raise brassica transplants yourself, if possible, to minimize the risk of bringing in disease.

Brassicas
Broad beans
Broccoli
Bromadiolone
Bromophos

Broad beans see **Beans**.

Broccoli see **Brassicas**.

Bromadiolone an anti-coagulant **rodenticide** used against **mice** and **rats**, which die slowly from dehydration caused by internal bleeding. It is a highly poisonous substance which will also kill humans (although only in large doses), along with other mammals and **birds**. For advice on safer, alternative methods of rodent control, see **Rats**.

Bromophos a non-**systemic insecticide** of the **organophosphorus** group, with a broad range of uses. It is slightly toxic, an **anticholinesterase** substance, and is harmful to wildlife, pets, and **bees**. Bromophos has a seven-day **harvest interval** and is moderately **persistent** in the **soil**. Try **cultural control**, biological control, **traps**, and **barriers** instead. Only resort to **natural insecticides**, such as **derris**, if all else fails.

Brown rot a serious fungal **disease** affecting most **tree fruit**. It causes soft brown patches to appear on the fruit, either while it is on the tree or in store. Dirty white pustules form later, usually in a concentric pattern, and the fruit may eventually shrivel. Small cankers may develop on spurs bearing the rotted fruit. Good **hygiene** is essential: remove and destroy infected fruit on the tree and prune out cankered spurs. Do not store damaged fruit.

BT see *Bacillus thuringiensis.*

Buckthorn common name given to two distinctive **shrubs** that are native to Britain: the alder buckthorn, *Frangula alnus*, and the purging buckthorn, *Rhamnus catharticus*. Both are suitable for planting in a mixed garden **hedge**. They also both have berries that are attractive to **birds**, and are the main food plants of the brimstone **butterfly**. They grow well in most garden **soils**, although alder buckthorn is less tolerant, preferring a fairly moist and sheltered site.

Buckwheat a useful annual **green manure** and a good **attractant plant**, *Fagopyrum esculentum*. It is fairly quick growing but not known for its **hardiness**. Sow it as a summer green manure. It is in a different plant family to any **vegetable**, so you can easily fit it into your crop **rotation**. Dig it in after two to three months, at any time before it flowers (see **Green manures** chart, pp. 80-1). However, if you can leave it longer, the tiny pink blooms will attract **hoverflies**.

Buddleia a garden **shrub**, *Buddleia davidii*, popularly known as the "butterfly bush"; the common **variety** has cones of perfumed mauve flowers. On a sunny day, these may be covered with **butterflies** and **bees**. There are varieties with flowers in different shades of purple or white, but not all of these are as attractive to butterflies. Buddleia bushes can grow straggly, but you can prevent this by hard **pruning**. They thrive in most well-drained **soils**, even fairly **alkaline** ones, but need a sunny position.

Bupirimate a **systemic fungicide**, used on a wide range of **fruit** and **vegetables**. It is mildly toxic, an eye, skin, and respira-

Brown rot
BT
Buckthorn
Buckwheat
Buddleia
Bupirimate

tory system **irritant**, with a **harvest interval** ranging from one day to two weeks. It is harmful to fish. Try **cultural control**, including good hygiene, instead.

Burgundy mixture a **copper fungicide** based on **copper sulphate** and sodium carbonate (washing soda). It is stronger than **Bordeaux mixture** and still accepted by organic gardeners. However, in the UK, its use by members of the Soil Association (see Useful Addresses, pp. 190-1) symbol scheme is only allowed in certain circumstances.

Bush fruit any type of soft **fruit** that grows on bushes. This category includes blackcurrants, redcurrants, white currants, and gooseberries, which are all worthwhile garden fruits that are becoming increasingly scarce to buy. They are fairly tolerant and produce good crops in most years. If you plant a range of **varieties**, you can be harvesting them over several months. They are all self-fertile, so other varieties are not needed for **pollination**.

Grow redcurrants, white currants, and gooseberries as bushes or, more decoratively, as half standards on stems of 1m (3ft 3in) in length. You can also train them into fans or cordons, which do not take up much space, and make picking easy. They will grow well in sun or light shade, although gooseberry blossom may be caught by **frost** on cold sites. Blackcurrants can only be grown as bushes, and need a much richer **soil** than most fruit and a sunny site.

You will probably need to use **netting** to protect bush fruit from **birds**. Alternatively, plant free-standing bushes in a **fruit cage**. **Aphids** and **sawfly** are **pests** of bush fruit. Powdery **mildew** is one of the commonest **diseases**, especially of gooseberries, but look out for **resistant varieties**. Blackcurrants are susceptible to **big bud**.

Butterflies important pollinators of plants and generally welcome in the garden. However, the larvae of a few species, notably the large and small white butterfly, are **pests** of **brassicas**, aptly named **cabbage caterpillars**. Despite this troublesome minority, you should encourage butterflies by choosing plants that are rich in nectar, such as **buddleia**, woodruff, candytuft, scabious, marjoram, and lavender. You will also need to provide food plants for their caterpillar young: both the red admiral and peacock larvae feed on **nettles**. See also **Pollination**.

Cabbage caterpillars any of the **caterpillars** that commonly feed on the leaves of **brassica** plants. There are at least three types: the yellow and black caterpillars of the large white butterfly; the smaller green caterpillars of the small white butterfly; and the plump, light green or brown caterpillars of the cabbage moth (see p. 17).

On small numbers of plants, you can control caterpillars by **handpicking**, particularly if you can spot the eggs. You can also prevent attacks by covering plants with a fine mesh **netting** – 1cm ($^2/_5$ in) square maximum. As a last resort, spray with *Bacillus thuringiensis*.

Cabbage root fly a fly whose small, white larvae feed on the roots of **brassicas**, usually causing the wilting and eventual death of young plants. Older plants can survive an attack, although the tunnels of the larvae may make **root crops**, such as turnips and swedes, inedible.

You can prevent damage to individual transplants by placing a mat of rubbery carpet underlay, 12.5cm (5in) square, around each one. This prevents the adult root fly from laying its eggs at the base of the stem. You can also protect closely spaced crops that you have sown directly in the **soil** by covering them with **fleece**. Dig over the soil in winter where a crop has been affected to expose the over-wintering **pests** to cold and **birds**.

You can also try **intercropping** brassica plants with other unrelated plants, planting out both crops when they are about the same size. Intercropping dwarf French **beans** and cabbages can work well, for example. Apparently this confuses the root fly so that it lays fewer eggs.

Cabbages see **Brassicas**.

Calciferol a **rodenticide**, used against **warfarin**-resistant **rats** and **mice**, often in mixtures with **difenacoum**. It is poisonous to humans, domestic animals, and wildlife, and may indirectly cause the death of animals and **birds** which eat poisoned rodents. For advice on safer, alternative methods of rodent control, see **Rats**.

Calcified seaweed a small red **seaweed**, *Lithothamnium calcareum*, more closely resembling a coral than other types of seaweed usually found on the shore. It contains large amounts of calcium carbonate, a source of **calcium**, with useful amounts of **magnesium** and a host of **trace elements**. In the garden, it is used as a soil conditioner and **compost activator** because it raises the soil **pH** and encourages the activity of **microorganisms**. However, it can concentrate any radioactivity in water. Its use by organic gardeners is being reviewed because of the ecological damage that may be caused by its collection.

Calcium an element, occurring in the **soil** in various forms, which is an essential **nutrient** for plant growth. Common forms of calcium include chalk, limestone, **dolomite**, and **gypsum**. **Egg shells** are a good source of calcium, which you can add to the **compost heap**, and certain **seaweed fertilizers** contain useful quantities of this nutrient. Calcium deficiency is unlikely in a well-managed organic garden, but plants are sometimes unable to distribute calcium through their systems, even though it is present in the soil, and may develop disorders, such as **blossom end rot**.

Californian poppy a hardy annual, *Eschscholzia californica*, which is a good **attractant plant** and popular with **bees**. Its flowers are usually shades of orange, appearing from early summer to autumn. It does best on a well-drained sunny site and, once established, will self-seed.

Calomel another name for **Mercurous chloride**.

Cane fruit
Canker
Capsid bugs
Captan

Cane fruit any type of soft **fruit** that produces woody stems, or canes. This category includes raspberries, blackberries, and the many valuable hybrid berries they have produced, for example, loganberries, boysenberries, and tayberries. Together these extend the soft-fruit season from July until the first autumn frosts. They are all very hardy, and crop reliably in cool areas (the exception being autumn-fruiting raspberries which need a long season). They are also self-fertile and so do not need other varieties for **pollination**.

Grow raspberries in a row with the canes supported by posts and wires. Or, in a small garden, plant a few around a central pole. Raspberries are slightly less tolerant than other cane fruit and do best in a sunny or partially shaded site on a light, rich **soil** that holds moisture. On **alkaline** soils they tend to suffer from **mineral deficiencies**. Cultivated blackberries rarely have the true flavour of those from the hedgerows, but they give heavy crops of large berries. You can train them against a **wall** or **fencing**, although they are vigorous so you will need to allow them plenty of room. The main **pests** of cane fruit are **birds**, **aphids**, and **raspberry beetle**, while cane spot, spur blight, **botrytis**, and **viruses** are the more troublesome **diseases**. It is worth buying **virus-free stock** and looking out for **resistant varieties**.

Canker see **Apple and pear canker** and **Parsnip canker**.

Capsid bugs a group of small, shield-shaped, winged bugs (see p. 17), some of which are garden **pests**. Plants that capsid pests commonly attack include most soft and **tree fruit**, **potatoes**, runner **beans**, **strawberries**, chrysanthemums, **asters**, **nasturtiums**, **buddleias**, roses, and a number of other **flowers** and **shrubs**.

Capsids are elusive so you may not spot them, but you will notice the damage they do. They leave irregular, ragged holes in leaves and distorted flowers and fruit. Plants can usually tolerate this damage: **apples**, for example, may be out of shape but they are still fit to eat and store. Capsid bugs can also transmit viral **diseases**, which may seriously harm plants. A few species of capsid, such as the black-kneed capsid, are **beneficial insects**, preying on mites, **aphids**, **caterpillars**, and other small pests.

Captan a powerful **fungicide** used alone or in mixtures to control **scab** on **apples** and pears, and **blackspot** on roses. It is highly poisonous and flammable, releasing toxic fumes when burnt. Captan is an eye, skin, and respiratory system **irritant**, and there is considerable evidence that it is a **carcinogen**, **teratogen**, and **mutagen**. Sweden and Finland both cited carcinogenic risks in their reasons for banning or severely restricting captan. This chemical is dangerous to a range of animals, (although apparently not to **bees** if used correctly), and is toxic to aquatic life. It is very **persistent** in the **soil**. Try **cultural control** instead.

Carbamates a group of **pesticides** including **insecticides**, **fungicides**, and **herbicides**. Carbamates are often **systemic** in their action. Although believed to be less hazardous than **organophosphorous** pesticides due to their short **persistence**, they are still highly toxic if inhaled, or absorbed through the skin. Some are suspect **carcinogens**.

Carbaryl an **insecticide**, growth regulator, and **earthworm** killer of the **carbamate** group. It is used against **capsid bugs**, **earwig**, and **caterpillar pests**. Carbaryl is a poison, an **anticholinesterase** compound, and there is evidence that it is a **carcinogen**, **mutagen**, and **teratogen**. Carbaryl is one of the **pesticides** that has been most responsible for **bee** deaths and it is also harmful to aquatic life at low concentrations. It is moderately **persistent** in the **soil**, and has a **harvest interval** of one to six weeks. There is no need to use chemical growth regulators and no reason to kill earthworms, which aerate the soil and keep it healthy.

Carbendazim a **systemic fungicide**, used on a wide range of moulds; it is a **metabolite** of **benomyl**. Carbendazim is moderately poisonous, an **irritant**, and there is limited evidence that it is a **carcinogen** and **mutagen**. Some pathogens show **resistance** to this chemical. Try **cultural control** instead.

Carbon-nitrogen ratio a measure of the proportionate amounts of carbon and **nitrogen** in any material. Ideally this should be roughly 30:1 in a newly formed **compost heap**, and 10:1 in fully matured compost. In practice, fibrous plant material supplies most of the carbon, while the nitrogen comes from **manure** and sappy plants, in particular **nettles**, **comfrey**, and **grass mowings**. Getting the ratio exactly right is not essential, but stemmy plant material will generally break down faster if you add nitrogen-rich substances, such as manure or **urine**. Conversely, manure or grass mowings will make better compost if mixed with fibrous material, such as **straw**.

Carcinogen any substance that can cause cancer. Known carcinogens include tobacco, **asbestos,** sunlight, radon, **bracken**, and various natural and artificial chemicals, including many **pesticides**.

There is no easy way to prove that something is carcinogenic. The two methods commonly used are laboratory tests on animals or bacterial cultures (toxicology), and studies on human populations which have been exposed to a particular, toxic substance (epidemiology). Neither method is foolproof.

Laboratory tests only show the impact of unnaturally large doses, and the fact that a particular species of animal shows increased risk of cancer after exposure does not necessarily mean that the same is true for humans, and vice versa. Epidemiological studies need to be carried out over long periods, because it can take 20 to 30 years or more for cancer to become obvious after exposure to a carcinogen; it is also extremely difficult to eliminate other possible causal factors. This is why there are so many "suspect" carcinogens. And even if something is known to be carcinogenic, the level of risk depends on how powerful a carcinogen it is, how often and how acutely you are exposed to it, and what other damaging substances you come into contact with. For example, cigarette smokers are more at risk from certain other carcinogens, such as asbestos dust, than non-smokers. On a garden scale, risks from most pesticides suspected of carcinogenity are probably very small, but not non-existent.

Similar problems are associated with the identification of **teratogens** and **mutagens**.

Cardboard a **biodegradable** material which has a variety of uses in **organic gardening**. Flattened cardboard boxes make good insulating lining for **compost bins**. They will also exclude light if used for **clearing ground**, although you need to weight them down well. If left in place, cardboard will eventually rot into the **soil**.

Carpet a useful material for **clearing ground** since it excludes light very effectively and is easy to secure with wire pegs.

Carcinogen
Cardboard
Carpet

Hessian-backed wool carpet is the best type to use since it will not leave residues of rubber behind. Carpet is also a good insulator. Use it to line **compost bins**, and put a piece across the top of the **compost heap** to keep the heat in and the rain out.

Carrot fly a fly whose larvae are a serious **carrot pest**; they also attack other **umbellifers** such as **celery, parsnips**, and parsley. The larvae feed on crop roots, killing seedlings and tunneling into older plants. Reddening leaves and stunted growth are visible symptoms of an attack, while tunneling can render carrots inedible.

An open-topped **barrier**, 75cm (30in) high, will protect carrots against this pest, because it is such a weak flier. Use **polythene** or a material with a very fine mesh to construct the barrier, which can be up to 3m (9ft 9in) long and 90cm (36in) wide. Alternatively, cover crops with **fleece** immediately after sowing, leaving this on until harvest time, if necessary.

The pest overwinters in the **soil** so you should dig over land that has had an affected crop to expose the pupae to **birds**. Adult flies emerge in May or June to lay their eggs near suitable crops, and a second generation appears in August or September. By delaying the **sowing time** until June, you can miss the first attack, and the carrots will be large and therefore less vulnerable by the second. **Intercropping** carrots and **onions** can sometimes help reduce damage since the carrot fly is deceived by the onion smell.

Carrots see **Root crops**.

Cat droppings see **Dog droppings**.

Caterpillars the larvae of **butterflies** and moths. Most feed on wild plants and do little damage, but a few are serious garden **pests**. This is particularly true of **cabbage caterpillars**, but also applies to the larvae of the **winter moth, codling moth**, and **pea moth**. On small numbers of plants, **handpicking** is the most effective way of dealing with these pests. The **biological control** *Bacillus thuringiensis* works well against some species, including cabbage caterpillars. As a last resort, try spraying with **derris**.

Cauliflowers see **Brassicas**.

Celery a **vegetable** grown mainly for its edible stems, although the leaves and seeds also have culinary uses. There are various different types of celery. Trench celery is the traditional winter crop, but it is not easy to grow well. Self-blanching celery is less trouble, but it is not so hardy. Leaf celery produces bushy plants, the leaves of which are used for seasoning and as a garnish.

Celery needs a **soil** rich in **organic matter** and plenty of moisture. It is an **umbellifer** so you should grow it with related crops, such as **carrots** and **parsnips**, in your **rotation**. Its main **pests** and **diseases** are **slugs**, **leaf miners**, celery heart rot, and celery **leaf spot**.

Cement a powdery mixture of **limestone** and clay, frequently combined with sand and water to form concrete and used, in the garden, for **path** laying and the construction of small buildings and **compost** pits. The cement used in concrete-making can act as an **irritant** so you should be careful to avoid getting it on your hands or breathing it in (see **Protective clothing**). Some cements have, in the past, contained **asbestos** so, when taking down or restoring old **walls**, you should treat any you come across with care.

Centipede an invertebrate with a segmented body (see p. 16), which you can distinguish from the **millipede** by the fact that the latter has two pairs of legs per segment while the centipede has only one. Various types of centipede are good **natural predators** of many garden **pests**, including **slugs**. You can encourage them in the garden by leaving large stones, logs, or loose **mulches** for them to hide under.

CFCs abbreviation of chlorofluorocarbons, a group of chemicals that cause damage to the **ozone** layer. Used in **aerosols**, refrigerators, and foam packaging, they are now being gradually phased out.

Chard see **Spinach**.

Cherry a **fruit** tree, with attractive blossom and a crop that you may have to share with the **birds**. Although traditionally trees for a large garden, there are now dwarfing **rootstocks** available, which you can train as fans or bushes in a smaller space. Sweet cherries like a warm, sunny site – a south-facing wall is ideal in cool regions – and usually need another variety for **pollination**. Acid cherries are more tolerant and also self-fertile. The main cherry **pests** are **blackfly**, **winter moth**, and **birds**, while **diseases** include **silver leaf** and **brown rot**.

Chicory see **Lettuce**.

Chilean nitrate a mixture of sodium and potassium nitrates, mined from Chilean desert deposits and used as a **natural fertilizer** in the garden. The use of Chilean nitrate is unacceptable in **organic gardening** both because it is a non-renewable resource and because it acts too quickly.

Chinese cabbage see **Brassicas**.

Chlordane an **organochlorine earthworm** killer, used mainly on turf. Chlordane is an extremely poisonous substance, and it is a suspect **carcinogen**, **mutagen**, and **teratogen**. It is highly dangerous to wild animals and **birds** and can last for up to 15 years in the **soil**. Chlordane has been banned in many countries and severely restricted within the European Community. There is no reason to kill beneficial **earthworms** – you need them in your **lawn** to keep the turf aerated and healthy.

Chlorofluorocarbons see **CFCs**.

Chloroxuron a soil-acting, urea-based **herbicide**, used for **weed control** around **strawberries** and chrysanthemums. It is not particularly poisonous but it is a mild eye, skin, and respiratory system **irritant**. Chloroxuron can cause damage to plants through **spray drift**. Try hand **weeding**, **hoeing**, or apply a **mulch** instead.

Chlorpyrifos an **insecticide** and **acaricide** of the **organophosphorus** group, used against a wide range of **pests**. It is poisonous and an eye and skin **irritant**. Chlorpyrifos is highly toxic to **birds**, **bees**, fish, and other wildlife, and can damage a number of plants. Try **cultural control**, **biological control**, **traps**, and **barriers** instead. Only resort to **natural insecticides**, such as **derris**, if all else fails.

Chocolate spot a common fungal **disease** of broad and field **beans**, which causes dark brown spots to appear on leaves, stems, flowers, and pods. It may result in reduced yields and severe attacks can kill plants. To reduce the likelihood of chocolate spot, grow beans on open, well-drained sites. Increase the **plant spacing** and the **potassium** levels in the **soil**. If this disease is a problem, avoid sowing during the autumn when beans are more susceptible and may carry over the infection.

Clay soil a heavy **soil type** which is difficult to work, being sticky when wet and tending to dry into hard lumps. Clay soils do not drain easily and this makes them slow to warm up in spring. However, they are usually rich in **nutrients** and potentially fertile.

To make clay soils easier to work, dig in plenty of **organic matter**, particularly long-lasting materials such as **leafmould**, which will improve the **soil structure**. They can then support a wide range of plants.

Clearing ground a method of clearing **weeds**, either by **cultivation** – forking, **digging**, or **rotavating** – or by using a **mulch** to exclude light from the **soil** and prevent plant growth.

Choose a method to suit the type of weed and the size of the area to be cleared. Forking and hand **weeding** will remove tap-rooted weeds, while digging and burying will get rid of unwanted annuals and shallow-rooted perennials. Both these methods are hard work, so save them for small areas of ground which you need for immediate use. Rotavating quickly clears annual weeds but it leaves chopped-up roots of persistent perennials, which may then regrow. To prevent this, rotavate several more times just as regrowth starts, at about three-week intervals.

Applying a mulch is the easiest and most effective way of clearing ground. Suitable materials include **cardboard**, black **polythene**, and **carpet**. You will need to keep the mulch in place for several months during the main growing season. Bear in mind that the deeper the roots of the weeds, the longer you will need to leave it.

Click beetle see **Wireworm**.

Climate the prevalent type of weather in a particular area. There is a lot you can do to mitigate the extent to which climatic extremes of cold, rainfall (or lack of it), and wind affect the plants in your garden. Begin by finding out what you can and cannot grow in terms of **hardiness**: note the plants growing around you that do best and choose ones that are similarly suited to local conditions. You can then implement various strategies: put up **windbreaks** and plant **hedges** to provide shelter; use **cloches** and **fleeces** to protect plants from **frost**; build **raised beds** for an early start on wet land; and allow for **irrigation**, where necessary.

Climbers plants that will cling, twine, or scramble up any support. You can use climbers to clothe bare **fencing** and **walls**, to cover arches and pillars, or to disguise an old shed. They will provide height and shelter for wildlife, of particular importance in a small garden where there is no room for **trees**. Try fitting supporting wires or trellis 5 to 7.5cm (2 to 3in) out from a wall so that there is space behind the screen for **birds** to nest and even a **bat** to roost.

There are climbers which will make the best of most situations – some will grow on shaded walls, for example, where fruit would not flourish. However, the **soil** at the base of a wall is usually poor and dry, so plant any climber at least 30cm (12in) away from it, digging in plenty of **organic matter**. Water the plant well until it is established.

Climbers
Cloches
Clover

Cloches removable covers of glass or **plastic** that you can use for protecting plants outdoors. Cloches are most useful early and late in the growing season when they will help to shelter tender plants from **frost**. You can also use them to raise the **soil temperature** for germinating seeds or for bringing on young seedlings, and to protect both from wind and heavy rain. Cloches ensure quicker growth and reduce the risk of **pest** and **disease** attack. You can either remove them once the plants are larger and less vulnerable, or with early crops of, say, **lettuce**, leave them on until harvest time. See also **Bottle cloches**.

Clover a plant with trifoliate leaves, several species of which are good **green manures**. They are all **legumes** and will fix **nitrogen** in the **soil**. Crimson clover, *Trifolium incarnatum*, is an annual, ready to dig in after two to three months in summer, although it may survive a mild winter. Essex red clover, *T. pratense*, is a short-lived perennial. Cut it down when it flowers to encourage new growth, and dig it in at any time when it is fresh and green. (See **Green manures** chart, pp. 80-1.)

Clubroot the most serious **disease** of **brassicas**, which also affects many related garden plants such as wallflowers and **mustard**, and some **weeds**. Roots become swollen and distorted and plants grow less strongly and may wilt and even die. Clubroot is a **soil**-borne disease, and once your soil has become contaminated there is little you can do – the fungus can survive there for 20 years or more.

Symptoms are most severe on poorly drained **acid soils**, so, to avoid problems, correct these conditions if necessary. Rather than risk bringing in infected transplants; raise your own. On infected land, you can try growing the few brassica varieties (of **swedes** and calabrese, for example) that are said to have some resistance to clubroot. You can also try raising all brassica plants in large pots so that they have a well-developed root system by the time you are ready to transplant them.

Codling moth a small moth, whose larvae are the familiar maggots you find in **apples**. They also occasionally attack **pears**. The larvae tunnel into the fruit in June or July and feed there for several weeks before leaving to pupate in crevices and cracks in the bark of the **tree**. They render fruit inedible and unsuitable for storing.

You can reduce codling moth numbers by using **traps** containing a synthetic sex attractant (pheromone). This lures male moths toward the sticky base of the trap. Hang the traps in the trees from mid May until about the end of July when the adults are most active. As a last resort, spray with **derris**. Use the traps to determine when to spray, starting seven to ten days after the first moths are caught.

Coir a fibrous material made from the coconut plant and added to **seed** and **potting composts**. Although used successfully as an alternative to **peat**, some types of coir may be treated with the highly toxic **methyl bromide**. Coir is imported from the Third World.

Cold frames structures traditionally built with low brick walls and sloping glass frames, used mainly for hardening off plants raised in the **greenhouse**. You can keep the frames propped open to provide ventilation, or remove them so that the plants become accustomed to outdoor conditions. You can also use cold frames for early sowings of crops, such as **radishes**, **lettuce**, and spring **onions**.

Colorado beetle a yellowish beetle, shaped like a **ladybird** but about twice the size, and with many longitudinal black stripes. It is a serious **pest** of **potatoes** and other crops, found in the USA and mainland parts of Europe, but not, so far, in Britain. It is an extremely voracious pest, with no **natural predators** in Britain, and so likely to spread very quickly if it ever became established. If you see a Colorado beetle, you should tell the police immediately. They will contact officials from the Ministry of Agriculture, who will try to eradicate it before it spreads.

Comfrey a hardy plant used as a **natural fertilizer**. You can make comfrey leaves into a **liquid feed**, dig them directly into the **soil**, or apply them as a **mulch**. Comfrey is also a good **compost activator**.

Russian comfrey, *Symphytum* x *uplandicum*, is the best type to use. Its leaves are rich in **potassium** (containing two to three times as much as **farmyard manure**) and are also a useful source of **nitrogen**, **phosphorus**, and other **minerals**. This plant cannot be grown from seed, but you can easily establish it from root **cuttings**. It is a vigorous grower, allowing you to harvest the leaves as many as three or four times in one season. To make a concentrated liquid feed, simply pack freshly picked leaves into a barrel with a drip hole underneath. Place a container under the hole to collect the resultant dark liquid, which you should dilute 10 to 20 times with water before use. If you dig the fresh leaves directly into the soil or apply them as a mulch, they will decay rapidly and quickly release their **nutrients**.

Compaction damage to the **soil structure**, resulting in airless, waterlogged conditions that are hostile to plant growth. Avoid walking on the **soil**, especially when it is wet, since this is one of the main causes of compaction. Growing plants on a **bed system** is one of the best ways of preventing this problem since you can carry out all work from the **paths**, without treading on the soil.

Companion planting a technique in which different species are planted close together for the benefit of one or both. The aim could be to keep away **pests** or **diseases**, or simply to help plant growth. You will find many companionships mentioned in books, for example, chives to protect roses from **blackspot**. Unfortunately, the recommendations tend

Colorado
beetle
Comfrey
Compaction
Companion
planting

43

to be contradictory and lacking in detail. Only one or two companionships have been shown to be significant, and these are not always practical. For example, sowing **carrots** among **onions** can keep **carrot fly** away, but only if you have four times as many onions as carrots and only while the onion tops are still green. **Intercropping** French **beans** and **cabbages** can sometimes reduce attacks by **cabbage root fly**, but you need to plan **sowing times** and harvesting dates carefully. The main benefit of any companionship is likely to be in increasing **diversity** in the garden and in attracting **beneficial insects**.

You could also regard the undersowing of main crops with **green manures** as a type of companion planting.

Compost

Compost activators

Compost bins

Compost a material formed from decomposed **vegetable** matter and, in most cases, animal **waste**. Compost is one of the best forms of **organic matter** for feeding the **soil**. You can make it in a **compost heap** or **tumbler** from plant debris and **household scraps**. As well as improving the **soil structure**, it provides **nutrients** in a well-balanced form. Good, well-matured compost is dark brown, crumbly, and pleasant to handle, but even rougher compost is useful. Do not confuse this garden compost with **seed** or **potting composts**, which you can buy or make for **plant raising**.

Compost activators substances that you can use to initiate the composting process. Many natural materials that are high in **nitrogen** are good activators, for example, **grass mowings**, **comfrey**, **urine**, and **nettles**. **Seaweed** is also useful. Most off-the-shelf activators contain chemical nitrogen, which is not acceptable in **organic gardening**. Others are herbal or bacterial preparations and while there is little scientific evidence to show that these work, some gardeners find them useful.

Compost bins containers for making **compost**, which you can either construct yourself or buy. As well as keeping a **compost heap** tidy, they should help to keep it moist and warm, and prevent rain from penetrating. You can make bins from **wood** (see **New Zealand box**), bricks, or **straw** bales, all of which are good insulating materials. If using wood, try to ensure that the **timber** comes from a sustainable source or reuse material (see **Recycling**), such as old floorboards or doors. Wooden boxes are also useful. Alternatively, use wire **netting** and line it with **carpet** or **cardboard**. A solid lid is best, although you can just place a square of carpet over the heap to help keep the heat in.

Compost heap a method of creating **compost** in the garden, in which you pile up layers of **biodegradable** plant debris and **household scraps** and allow them to decompose. You can either cover the heap with old **carpet** or build it up within a **compost bin**. A bin does look neater and can give you better conditions for composting.

Most **waste** materials of living origin can go on a compost heap (see chart overleaf). This way you can recycle them back to the **soil** rather than throwing them away. Keep a separate bucket for compost material in your kitchen, for example, and use a **shredder** to chop woody **prunings** for inclusion in the heap. Ideally, a heap needs a mixture of sappy, **nitrogen**-rich materials, such as **grass mowings**, and fibrous ones, for example, flower stems. If you do not have enough sappy materials, you need to add a **compost activator**. If you have too many, you will need to bring in tougher materials, such as **straw**; these also help to keep air in the heap. Compost materials should be moist but not soaking wet.

Compost heap

The decomposition process is carried out by living organisms. Initially, **aerobic bacterial decomposition** occurs and this causes the heap to heat up. With the right conditions, you can get temperatures over 140°F (60°C), which will kill many **weed** seeds and **disease** organisms. As the air is used up and the heap cools, other creatures become active as well and decomposition becomes slower. You can speed it up by turning the heap to let air in and by adding extra materials to correct the **carbon-nitrogen ratio**.

There are several reasons why a compost heap may not produce good compost quickly. If the heap dries out or loses a lot of heat, decomposition will be very slow. This often happens in a small heap, which has a large surface area as compared to its volume. Heaps smaller than 1m (3ft 3in) cubed need a lot of insulation to work well. Similarly, decomposition will be slow if you make up a heap bit by bit and never allow heat the chance to build up. Finally, if the heap is too wet, air will be driven out and **anaerobic bacterial decomposition** will occur, producing a slimy, foul-smelling material. See also **Tumbler** and **Trench composting** for alternative composting methods. ▷

What goes on a compost heap ?

Material	Comment
Autumn leaves	Add enough to make up roughly 10% of the heap, but keep large amounts for making **leafmould**.
Comfrey leaves	Use as a **compost activator**.
Diseased plant material	A hot heap should kill many disease organisms but not the persistent ones, such as **clubroot**. If in doubt, burn or put diseased material in the dustbin.
Flower and **vegetable** debris	These should be the principal ingredients of the heap, but see cautions on using diseased material and weeds. Chop up tough flower stems and **brassica** stalks, or use a **shredder**.
Grass mowings	Use as a compost activator.
Hair clippings	Add small amounts since it takes a long time to decompose.
Household scraps: **fruit** and vegetable peelings, **egg shells**, and tea leaves	Mix with other materials, but exclude meat and fish scraps if **rats** are a problem. You can also add **kitchen waste** direct to a **wormbin**.
Manure	Strawy manure will add bulk to the heap. Strawless manures, such as that of poultry, are good activators.
Paper	Add small amounts, torn into pieces. Avoid paper marked in coloured inks.
Prunings and hedge clippings	Chop up by hand or with a **shredder** before including.
Seaweed	Use as a compost activator.
Soil	Too much of this slows up the composting process, so shake plant roots and do not add extra soil.
Straw	Break up before adding and water if dry.
Weeds	Most are useful composting materials, but do not add roots of persistent weeds, such as couch grass, or large tap roots, such as dock, unless you have dried them out well in the sun first.
Wood ash	Small amounts will provide **potassium** and **lime**. Do not include coal or other ashes.

Compost heap (chart)

46

Compost toilet a unit designed to **compost** human **waste** for use as a **natural fertilizer**. The waste is stored in aerobic conditions and, if the process works correctly, gradually transforms into a friable, odourless, **soil**-like substance over a period of months. Most compost toilets need to be placed over a large and accessible pit in which decomposition can take place, although smaller units have been developed which use heaters to speed up the composting process. Unfortunately, compost toilets have not so far proved effective in destroying some of the more persistent **bacteria** and other **disease** pathogens, so you still should not use composted human waste on food crops.

Concrete see **Cement**.

Conservatory an "add-on" room, usually made of glass, and attached to the sun-facing side of the house. In theory, a well-planned conservatory will maximize solar gain for most of the year and remain warm in winter by using **waste** heat from inside the house. Thus, it employs the same design techniques as a passive **solar greenhouse**. Unfortunately, in practice, many designs for conservatories are costly to install and not particularly **energy** efficient, so you should plan yours carefully to avoid this.

Contact pesticide any chemical which kills quickly on touching a **pest**, **disease** pathogen, or **weed**. See also **Systemic pesticide** and **Translocated herbicide**.

Convolvulus, annual a low-growing hardy annual, *Convolvulus tricolor*, which is a good **attractant plant**, especially for **hoverflies**. **Bees** also love the blue flowers, which appear in summer and early autumn. It grows best on a well-drained, sunny site.

Copper fungicides a group of **fungicides** used against **fungi**, including moulds, and generally regarded as having low toxicity to humans, although this does not mean that they are harmless. Some copper fungicides pose a risk to animals, and users should keep poultry or livestock out of treated areas for three weeks following application. They are also harmful to fish. Copper in itself is **persistent** in the **soil** and can harm some plants. Two members of this group, **Bordeaux mixture** and **Burgundy mixture**, both based on

Create a healthy and productive food garden, keeping to the guidelines given below.

Herbs For easy access, plant culinary **herbs**, such as chives, mint, fennel, and rosemary near to the house. Most of these attract **bees** and **beneficial insects**.

Greenhouse A small **greenhouse** is ideal for **plant raising**, enabling you to start plants off in the warmth. This makes them less vulnerable to **pest** and **disease** attack. In summer, use the space for tender crops, such as **tomatoes** and **peppers**. (See pp. 50-1 for tips on design and planting of a **solar greenhouse**.)

Water butt This enables you to collect water for **irrigation** from the greenhouse roof.

Bed system Growing **vegetables** on a four-year **rotation** will help control pests and diseases and make the best use of **soil fertility**. Plot A contains **potatoes**; plot B **root crops**; plot C **brassicas**; and plot D **peas**, **beans**, and crops of the marrow family. Each plot is divided into narrow beds which you can cultivate from the **paths** so that you never need to tread on the **soil**. You can use various **barriers** against pests, such as the **fleece** covering the carrots in plot B to protect them from **carrot fly**. The **green manure** crop of **mustard** on plot C should be dug in when kale and broccoli are ready to be planted. **Cloches** on plot D help the emergence of French **bean** seeds.

Fruit trees To save on space, you can train **apples** and **pears** as

espaliers and **plums** as fans. The **varieties** to choose are those that are less susceptible to pests and diseases. Fruit trees also need careful selection to ensure that cross-**pollination** occurs.

Fruit cage This will protect **bush** and **cane fruit** (raspberries, redcurrants, black currants, and gooseberries) from the **birds**. Choose varieties to provide you with a range of fruit throughout the season and also those that show some resistance to pests and diseases.

Flowerbeds The beds contain annual and perennial **attractant plants** and some edible flowers, such as **nasturtiums**. If you have space, include ornamental, perennial vegetables, such as globe **artichokes**.

Fence A semi-solid **fence** is best for wind protection. You can make use of it to train cane fruit and ornamental **climbers**.

Comfrey patch An area reserved for this herb provides leaves for making **liquid feed**, and for use as a **mulch** or **compost activator.**

Leafmould bins Use these bins for rotting down autumn leaves.

Compost bins Wooden bins provide good insulation. Turn a completed **compost heap** from one bay to the next to aerate it, and then leave it to mature while you start another.

Manure Use bought-in **stable manure** and cover it with a plastic sheet to prevent the rain washing out **nutrients**.

49

Wormbin

Ventilation holes

Well-fitting lid

Wet newspaper

Vegetable scraps

Worms in bedding material: leafmold or shredded newspaper

Wooden partition: either planks or piece of wood with holes

Gravel

Drainage holes

1 Sunken beds

2 Trickle system

3 Annual climbers

4 Pot plants in hanging baskets

5 Double-glazed roof and external walls

6 Tender vegetables in small pots

7 Seed trays

8 Insulated walls and floors

9 Shade-loving plants

10 Roof and floor vents

11 Grapevine

12 Roller blinds or shutters

13 Small tender shrubs

14 Recycled shelving and staging

Prunings You can put these through a **shredder** for use as a mulch or for inclusion in the compost heap.

Windbreak Create a plantation of **trees** and **shrubs** as a protective shelter, including many which provide food for humans and wildlife, such as damsons and **crab apple. Coppicing hazels** will give you long, straight poles as pea sticks.

Beehives Place these in a sheltered, sunny position.

Store Keep this dry and aerated for storing **fruit** and vegetables.

Wormbin A medium-sized **wormbin**, placed close to the back door, is ideally situated for disposing of **kitchen waste**. To get the composting process going, you will need between 50 and 100 **brandling worms** and suitable bedding material, such as leafmould. Cover the bin to keep the contents moist.

Lean-to solar greenhouse

To maximize on solar gain throughout the year, position your lean-to **greenhouse** as near to south facing as possible, with the glass roof sloping at an angle of between 40° and 50°. If you can, use sustainable **timber** in its construction. A passive **solar heating** system will provide ideal conditions for plant growth, as well as helping to warm the house in winter.

Double-glazed roof and external walls These will absorb and retain the sun's heat.

Roller blinds or shutters Choose well-insulated blinds or shutters for summer shade and to conserve heat during cooler winter months.

Insulated walls and floors Dark brick or stone walls and floors absorb the sun's heat, releasing it at night or during overcast weather. You can improve their insulating capacity by covering them with plaster or tiles.

Roof and floor vents Roof vents are essential for releasing excess heat in summer. Use the floor vents to let cool air in.

Recycled staging/shelving Old wooden boxes, tables, and chairs can all provide a useful source of timber for shelving.

Trickle system Place this along the base of plants, covered with a **mulch**, to provide a carefully regulated supply of water for **irrigation**.

Seed trays Keep this area for germinating vegetable and flower seeds.

Pot plants in hanging baskets Fuchsias and geraniums thrive in the greenhouse, protected from wind and **frost**.

Small tender shrubs Many **herbs**, such as bay and lemon verbena, are susceptible to the cold and wet and best grown in pots for putting out in summer.

Tender vegetables Start off tender **vegetables**, such as **courgettes**, **sweetcorn**, and **marrows** in pots for cropping in the border over the summer.

Shade-loving plants Use the floor space under the staging for shade-loving foliage plants.

Sunken beds Sunken beds are ideal for plants that you want to grow inside all year round. Here, **tomatoes** thrive against a sun-facing wall.

Annual climbers Train annual **climbers**, such as morning glory, up the walls to add colour and attract **beneficial insects**.

Grapevine A vine spreading upward under the slanting glass roof will provide dappled shade and a crop of grapes within easy reach at harvest time.

copper sulphate, are used by organic gardeners, but only as last resorts when **cultural control** has failed.

Copper naphthenate a **copper fungicide** and ingredient of some **wood preservatives**. It is highly toxic if swallowed or inhaled. Although considered relatively safe for use with **bats**, the solvents it contains may be harmful and should not be used where bats are roosting.

Copper sulphate the main constituent of **Bordeaux mixture**, a **copper fungicide**.

Coppicing the practice of cutting **trees** off at the stump to encourage many smaller shoots to grow rather than one main trunk. Traditionally, coppicing was practised to provide a ready source of firewood. Coppiced **ash** trees grow straight poles, which make good **fencing** material.

Cotoneaster any shrub of the genus *Cotoneaster*. All of the popularly grown species are good for wildlife. They have masses of small white flowers, loved by **bees**, followed by red berries which are attractive to **birds**. There are low-growing forms which make excellent **ground cover**, and you can train others against a **wall** or plant them as a **hedge**. Cotoneasters grow well in most garden **soils**, either in sun or partial shade.

Coumatetalryl an anticoagulant **rodenticide** used against **rats**. Coumatetalryl can also affect **birds**, wild and domestic animals, and children, if they get hold of it. For safer, alternative methods of rodent control, see **Rats**.

Courgettes see **Squashes**.

Cover crop a crop whose foliage covers the ground densely, binding the soil to prevent **erosion** and preventing **nutrients** from washing away. Ideally, you should grow a cover crop on all spare **vegetable** plots during the winter, either a **green manure** or a hardy leafy crop, such as **spinach**.

Crab apple a small **tree** of the genus *Malus*, native to Britain, of which there are many cultivated garden forms. They are popular for their attractive blossom. **Birds** and other creatures enjoy the fruit, and you can also use the flowers for making jelly or wine. The trees grow best on well-drained **soil** in full sun.

Creosote a **wood preservative** used on outdoor **timber**, including garden **fencing** and **furniture**. It is poisonous if swallowed, inhaled, or absorbed through the skin, and is strongly suspected of being a **carcinogen**. Creosote has been banned from any but professional use in the USA, although their product is substantially different to that used in the UK. Never use creosote on **bird** or **bat** boxes since it can kill the inhabitants. Likewise, do not use it to treat fencing which plants are to climb. It is questionable whether it is worth using at all, but if you do employ it, always wear **protective clothing**, avoid breathing in fumes, and never smoke or use a naked flame nearby since it is flammable. Keep children and pets well away when applying. See **Timber treatment** for safer alternatives.

Creosote
Cresylic acid
Cucumber

Cresylic acid a **contact fungicide**, **soil** sterilant, and **insecticide**, used against **honey fungus** and **canker** on **trees**, overwintering **pests** on **fruit**, and **ants**, **slugs**, and **woodlice** in **greenhouses**. It is also used to keep **paths** clear of **moss** and **weeds**. Cresylic acid is an eye, skin, and respiratory system **irritant**, and dangerous to fish. It remains active in the **soil** for some months and can cause damage to other plants through **spray drift**. Try **cultural control** to prevent fungal attack. Alternatives for containing pests include **cultural control**, **biological control**, **barriers**, and **traps**, and as a last resort, **natural insecticides**, such as **derris**. Use hand **weeding** or a **mulch** for clearing paths.

Cucumber a tender plant grown for its fleshy fruit. Some types will only thrive in a **greenhouse**, but ridge cucumbers will grow outside in a sunny, sheltered spot; they produce short fruit with prickly skins in contrast to the smoother greenhouse **varieties**. All prefer a **soil** rich in **organic matter** and containing plenty of moisture. Most cucumbers grow on long vines, so you can train them on canes or trellis and use the space beneath for **intercropping**. Grow them with **squashes** in your crop **rotation**.

Greenhouse cucumbers need high temperatures 50°F (10°C) or above, so do not sow them until late spring in cold regions. The fruit of these varieties becomes bitter if pollinated, so it is well worth getting hold of modern ones that produce only female flowers. Cucumbers are prone to **cucumber mosaic virus** and powdery **mildew**, but look out for **resistant varieties**. The most troublesome pests are **slugs**, **aphids**, and **red spider mites**.

Cucumber mosaic virus a common and widespread **disease** that affects **celery**, **lettuce**, **spinach**, and many **flowers** and **weeds**, as well as plants in the **cucumber** family. Symptoms include stunted plant growth, yellow mottled leaves, and distorted flowers and fruit. The disease is generally transmitted by **aphids**. You should grow **resistant varieties** where available – there are, for example, some such varieties of **marrows** and **courgettes**. Remove weeds, such as chickweed, that act as overwintering hosts, and dig up and destroy infected plants.

Cucumber mosaic virus
Cultivation
Cultural control

Cultivation the preparation of ground to encourage plant growth. Some cultivation of the **soil** by **digging**, **rotavating**, forking, **hoeing**, and raking is necessary to aerate the **soil** and, in some cases, to prevent **weed** growth, but you should take care not to over cultivate. Excessive digging, forking, and rotavating can easily damage the **soil structure**. Never cultivate when the soil is very wet or frozen since this can be particularly harmful.

Cultural control a technique used in **organic gardening**, which makes use of particular growing methods for controlling **pests** and **disease**. Creating good **soil** conditions by improving the **soil fertility** and **soil structure** is important as is choosing the right site for a particular plant or crop, since plants growing in inappropriate conditions will be weaker and thus more prone to problems. You should also practise good garden **hygiene** at all times, removing infected plants and debris that may pass on pests and diseases. Plan your **rotation** so that **vegetable** crops move around the garden from year to year. There are other techniques you can use to overcome specific problems: using **resistant varieties** that are less susceptible to certain pests and diseases; adjusting **sowing times** to miss the periods when a particular pest is at its most troublesome; and regulating the soil **pH** in an attempt to reduce the severity of some of the more damaging diseases, such as **scab** and **clubroot**.

In the case of fungal **disease**, should cultural controls, such as good hygiene, rotation, and the use of resistant varieties, fail to prevent or control an attack, you can use the **copper fungicide**, **Bordeaux mixture**, but only do so as a last resort.

Currants see **Bush fruit**.

Cuttings a method of **plant raising** which is useful for multiplying **shrubs**, and **bush fruit**. However, you should only use this method if you are sure that the parent plant is healthy since cuttings taken from **virus**-infected plants will carry over the **disease**. The **rooting powders** frequently used on cuttings are unacceptable in **organic gardening**.

Cutworms the plump, soil-living **caterpillars** (see p. 17) of various types of moth that are common garden **pests**. They vary in colour, but are often brown, yellow, or green. Cutworms feed at night, severing young plants at ground level, and will often work their way along a row. They also feed on the roots and tubers of crops such as **celery**, **carrots**, **beetroot**, **potatoes**, and **strawberries**.

Always search in the **soil** around a young plant that has just been severed – you will often find the cutworm that is responsible. You can protect individual plants with a collar of tin or plastic drainpipe, pressed down about 5cm (2in) into the **soil**. Attacks are often worst during periods of drought, and **irrigation** can help reduce damage. In plots where a crop has been affected, **digging** to expose overwintering cutworms may help reduce numbers.

Cypermethrin a **contact insecticide** of the **pyrethroid** group, used against a wide range of **pests**. It is poisonous if swallowed or absorbed through the skin, an eye and skin **irritant**, and there is some evidence that, at very high doses, it may be **oncogenic** and a **carcinogen**. Cypermethrin is dangerous to **bees** and is noted for its ruthless efficiency in killing **butterflies** and moths. It is also hazardous to aquatic life, even at the low concentrations that may occur following **spray drift** and it may damage some ornamental plants. It is flammable. Try **cultural control**, **biological control**, **traps**, and **barriers** instead. Only resort to the use of **natural insecticides**, such as **derris**, if all else fails.

2,4-D a **translocated herbicide**, used alone or in mixtures for general **weed control**; some formulations are designed specifically for use on turf or near water. 2,4-D is a poison and highly irritating to the eyes and skin. It is hazardous to animals, and in the USA it is recommended that no grazing be allowed on treated ground for two weeks following its use. **Spray drift** is a particular problem because 2,4-D is volatile and can evaporate and affect other plants nearby even if there is no wind at the original time of spraying. New turf and plants sown on recently treated ground may also suffer damage. Try hand **weeding**, **hoeing**, forking, or apply a **mulch**, instead.

Dalapon a **translocated herbicide** employed against **weeds**, such as couch grass, and sedges near water; it is either used alone or in mixtures with, for example, **2,4-D**. Dalapon is a corrosive poison, causing severe irritation of the mouth and stomach if swallowed, although it is unlikely to be fatal. It is an **irritant** to the eyes and may also affect the skin. **Spray drift** can cause damage. Try applying a **mulch**, or forking, which will remove the roots of couch grass.

Daminozide a growth regulator for use on **apple trees**. Researchers in the USA identified daminozide **residues** on apples as being **carcinogens**. A campaign against its use resulted in its being withdrawn in New Zealand, the USA, and several other countries, but not in Britain. It has now been withdrawn from sale worldwide, so you are no longer likely to buy apples or apple juice containing its residues. See also **Residues, pesticide**.

Damping off a common fungal **disease** of seedlings, which causes them to rot at the base and to die out in patches. Good **hygiene** is essential: wash seed boxes and pots, and clean out **water butts** regularly. Use a good **seed compost**, and make sure that it does not become waterlogged.

Deep bed gardening see **Bed system**.

Degradation product a product of the breakdown of a substance, for example, a **pesticide**. Although degradation products are intended to be harmless, they can be more hazardous than the parent chemical. Those resulting from the burning of pesticides are frequently harmful.

Deltamethrin a **contact insecticide** with residual activity, belonging to the **pyrethroid** group; it is used alone and in mixtures. Deltamethrin is a poison, and users are advised to wear **protective clothing** since it may be absorbed through the skin. It is dangerous to **bees** (although they are said to be repelled by this chemical), and to fish and other aquatic life. Deltamethrin is flammable. Try **cultural control**, **biological control**, **traps**, and **barriers** instead. Only resort to **natural insecticides**, such as **derris**, if all else fails.

Demeton-s-methyl a **systemic** and **contact insecticide** and **acaricide** of the **organophosphorus** group, used widely against insect **pests**, including **red spider mites**. It is poisonous if swallowed, inhaled, or absorbed through the skin, and there is some evidence that it is a **mutagen**. Users are advised to wear **protective clothing**. It is harmful to wild and domestic animals and to **birds**, and there is a **harvest interval** of up to three weeks. Some red spider mites are **resistant** to this chemical. Try **cultural control**, **biological control**, **barriers**, and **traps** instead, only resorting to **natural insecticides**, such as **derris**, if all else fails.

Dermatitis a skin inflammation which may be brought on by **allergens**, **irritants**, and other sensitizing materials; also known as eczema. If you are susceptible to dermatitis, take special care to avoid contact with irritant chemicals.

Derris a **natural insecticide** derived from the root of a tropical plant, *Derris eliptica*; also known as rotenone. It is poisonous, a mild skin **irritant**, and a suspected **mutagen** and **teratogen**. Derris is harmful to insects, wildlife, and fish, and has moderate **persistence**. It is one of the few insecticides passed for use by organic gardeners due to its relatively short persistence. Only resort to derris if you have failed to control **pests** by **cultural control, biological control, barriers**, or **traps**. Applications will certainly kill some **natural predators**, including **beneficial insects**.

Design, garden the underlying framework and accompanying planting schemes that characterize a garden. In **organic gardening**, designs aim to establish an ecological balance in the garden by including as much **diversity** as possible, evidenced both in the hard features and in the planting schemes. Plan to have a **pond** and at least one **tree** if you can since both of these create additional **microclimates** in the garden; you might also include a rockery or a drystone **wall**. Simply combining plants with different growing habits, or managing them in different ways, will also help: an area of long grass in addition to a **lawn**, **climbers** as well as **ground cover plants**, and dense **shrubs** together with an annual border.

With **vegetables** and **fruit**, try to get as far away from a **monoculture** as possible by growing a range of different crops. You also need to allow space for making **compost**, stacking **manure**, using a **shredder**, and growing **comfrey**, for example. Remember you have no weedkillers so establish firm foundations for **paths**, patios, and other features with this in mind. Above all, make sure that plants have the right growing conditions – by putting up **windbreaks**, for example – because only then will they thrive.

Diazinon an **insecticide** and **acaricide** of the **organophosphorus** group, used especially against **cabbage root fly**, **carrot fly**, and mushroom fly. It is poisonous and an **anticholinesterase** substance. Both diazinon vapour and the fumes released when it is heated are hazardous to health: its inappropriate use on house plants has poisoned users. Many studies suggest that diazinon may be a **teratogen**. It is dangerous to animals and very damaging to aquatic life – growth of some freshwater invertebrates has been depressed by as little as 0.003 parts per billion of diazinon in water.

Dicamba a **translocated herbicide** used in mixtures against a wide range of broad-leaved **weeds**. It is an **irritant** and suspected **mutagen**. **Spray drift** may also be a problem. Try hand **weeding**, **hoeing**, and, in the case of long-rooted perennial weeds, regular forking.

Dichlobenil a soil-acting **herbicide** used for total **weed control** on uncultivated land, **paths**, and patios, and also selectively around certain plants, in particular water **weeds**. It is an eye, skin, and respiratory system **irritant**, and research in the USA found that prolonged exposure to it could lead to chloracne, a severe skin complaint. It can be harmful to fish, and **spray drift** can cause serious damage, particularly in the case of young rose bushes and **raspberries**. Try hand **weeding**, **hoeing**, forking, or apply a **mulch** to clear **weeds** from paths.

Dichlofluanid a **fungicide** used to control mould on soft **fruit** and **mildew** on **cauliflower**. It is poisonous, an eye, skin, and respiratory system **irritant**, and there is some evidence that it is a **mutagen**. Dichlofluanid is moderately **persistent** and has a **harvest interval** ranging from three days to three weeks. It is hazardous to fish. Try **cultural control** instead.

Dichlorophen a **contact herbicide**, used especially to control **moss** on **lawns**. It is moderately toxic and may be inhaled or absorbed through the skin. It is harmful to fish. See **Lawn maintenance** for alternative methods of moss control.

Dichlorprop a **translocated herbicide**, used alone or in mixtures against a range of broad-leaved **weeds**. It is an eye, skin, and respiratory system **irritant**, and **spray drift** can cause damage, especially when dichlorprop is combined with **MCPA**. Try hand **weeding**, **hoeing**, or apply a **mulch**.

Dichlorvos an **insecticide** and **acaricide** of the **organophosphorus** group, used on a range of **fruit** and **vegetables**. It is especially favoured in **greenhouses** because of its short **persistence** and is frequently used before harvesting as a quick method of killing **pests**. It is, however, one of the most hazardous **pesticides**, being highly poisonous, an **anticholinesterase** compound, and an eye, skin, and respiratory system **irritant**. It is toxic to animals, **birds**, **bees**, and fish. It can damage some plants, including **cucumbers**, chrysanthemums, and roses. Try **cultural control**, **biological control**, **traps**, and **barriers** instead. Only resort to **natural insecticides**, such as **derris**, if all else fails.

Dicoful an **organochlorine acaricide** used alone or in mixtures against mites, including **red spider mites**, on **fruit** and **vegetables**. It is poisonous and may be absorbed through the skin, and there is evidence that it is an animal **carcinogen**. It may be hazardous to fish. Dicoful is **persistent** in the **soil**, with a **harvest interval** ranging from two to twenty one days, depending on the crop. Some strains of red spider mite show **resistance** to this chemical.

Difenacoum a **rodenticide** used to kill **mice** and **rats**, often in mixtures with **calciferol**. It is poisonous. For safer, alternative methods of rodent control, see **Rats**.

Dicoful
Difenacoum
Digging
Dimethoate

Digging turning of the **soil** with a spade. You may need to dig for a number of reasons: to break the soil down and get air into it; to bury **organic matter**, **green manures**, or **weeds**; to expose **pests** to the cold and to **birds**; or to allow clods of heavy soil to be weathered by the elements.

The double digging method, in which the soil is loosened to two spades depth, is worth adopting if **compaction** is a problem or if your soil is draining badly. It can also be a useful method for **clearing ground** of annual and shallow-rooted perennial weeds. However, digging is not always necessary or desirable, particularly on a light soil. It disturbs the **soil structure** and encourages the loss of moisture and organic matter. In theory, if a soil is in good condition, you can grow food crops and **flowers** without digging at all, adding any organic matter as a **mulch** and scraping it away when you need to sow or plant. In practice, a compromise works well: avoid routine digging, only turning the soil when really necessary, for example, to bury green manures or to create a seedbed on heavy soils.

Dimethoate a **systemic insecticide** and **acaricide** of the **organophosphorus** group used to control a wide range of **pests** on **vegetables**, **fruit**, and **flowers**. It is a poison, an **anticholinesterase** compound, and there is some evidence that it is an animal **carcinogen**. Dimethoate has been restricted in the USA, where permitted users are advised to wear **protective clothing**, and according to the US Environmental

Protection Agency there is evidence that it is a **mutagen**. Dimethoate is fairly **persistent** in the **soil**, with a **harvest interval** of one week. Try **cultural control, biological control**, **traps**, and **barriers** instead. Only resort to **natural insecticides**, such as **derris**, is all else fails.

Dinocap a non-**systemic fungicide** used to control powdery mildew on **fruit, vegetables**, and **flowers**. It is a poison, an eye, skin, and respiratory system **irritant** (and can stain the skin and hair), and has been identified as a possible **mutagen**. It has a **harvest interval** of one week and is toxic to fish.

Diquat a **contact herbicide**, often used in mixtures with **paraquat**. It is an extremely hazardous poison, an eye and skin **irritant**, and there is evidence that some forms of it are **mutagens** and **teratogens**. Try hand **weeding, hoeing**, forking, or apply a **mulch**.

Dirty Dozen Pesticides a list of highly dangerous **pesticides** which the International Pesticides Action Network (see Useful Addresses, pp. 190-1) is campaigning to have banned throughout the world. Since its creation the list has been expanded to include the following 18 chemicals: aldicarb, aldrin, campheclor, **chlordane**, chlordimeform, dibromochloroprophane, dieldrin, DDT, endrin, ethyl parathion, ethylene dibromide, **gamma HCH** (also known as lindane), heptachlor, parathion ethyl, parathion methyl, **paraquat, pentachlorphenol**, and **2,4,5-T**. In the UK, the only ones likely to be found in gardens are chlordane, gamma HCH, paraquat, pentachlorphenol, and 2,4,5-T.

Disease any impairment of a plant's health caused by **fungi, bacteria**, or **viruses**.

Disease control any measure taken to prevent fungal, bacterial, or viral **disease** pathogens harming garden plants. Fungal disease is conventionally treated with chemical **fungicides**. In an organic garden, these are unacceptable. Instead, you should follow the guidelines given under **cultural control**, which is also the most effective method for preventing and containing bacterial and viral attacks.

Diversity the principle that a garden should contain as many different plants and **habitats** for wildlife as is feasible. The greater the diversity, the more likely it is that a natural balance will be maintained between all creatures in the garden, and the less likely it is that any **pest** or **disease** will reach damaging levels. In addition to planting a wide variety of **vegetables**, **fruit**, **shrubs**, **herbs**, and **flowers**, you can introduce elements, such as **trees** and **ponds**, which create their own **microclimates**, and practise **rotation** and **intercropping**. **Monoculture** – the practice of growing a single crop in the same plot year after year – is the enemy of natural diversity. It allows crop-specific **pests** and **diseases** to build up, and upsets the **nutrient** balance of the **soil**.

DNOC a **contact insecticide** and **acaricide**, used to control over-wintering **aphids**, **scale insects**, **red spider mites**, and other **pests**. It is very poisonous if swallowed and harmful if absorbed through the skin. DNOC is dangerous to animals, **birds**, and fish and is more toxic to **soil** invertebrates than most insecticides. It is moderately **persistent** in the soil. Approvals for its use have been withdrawn in the UK, so it should no longer be on sale. Try **cultural control**, **biological control**, **traps**, and **barriers** instead. Only resort to **natural insecticides**, such as **derris**, if all else fails.

Dog droppings the faeces of dogs, a high proportion of which are infected with the parasite toxocariasis. This parasite is also found in cat droppings. If ingested by humans, it can cause serious, long-term health effects, including blindness. It is estimated that about a hundred British children suffer permanent eye damage every year as a result of toxocariasis. Make sure that no droppings are left on the grass or soil where children play. Many European countries insist that dog owners carry a trowel-like implement for scooping up faeces for proper disposal.

Dogwood a **shrub** of which the species, *Cornus sanguinea*, is native to Britain, with attractive red stems and black berries that are loved by the **birds**. It will grow well in most **soils**, either in sun or light shade. Dogwood can grow quite large but you can restrict it by severe **pruning**.

Dolomite a type of **lime**stone, which contains **magnesium** as well as **calcium**. It is slow acting and a useful way to raise **pH** in **acid soil**. You can also use it effectively for long-term correction of **magnesium** deficiency.

DNOC
Dog droppings
Dogwood
Dolomite

Double digging see **Digging**.

Drainage any method of getting rid of surplus water to prevent waterlogging and damage to **soil fertility**. A **soil** needs draining if puddles lie on the surface for a long period after rain or if holes that you dig fill with water. Surface water may be due to a heavy top soil, in which case the best solution is to dig in **organic matter**. **Compaction** of the soil a few inches below the surface can also prevent water from infiltrating. You can usually break a compacted layer up by **digging**. If the problem originates further down in the subsoil, you will need some kind of artificial drainage. In a small garden, you can dig simple trenches, 30-45cm (2-3ft) deep. Fill them with gravel or rubble before replacing the soil.

Drought gardening see **Water conservation**.

Dutch elm disease a fungal **disease** of **elms**. It is carried by bark beetles which fly from tree to tree. In England over the last twenty years, the rural landscape has changed dramatically due to the death of native elms from this disease. For some time, the Wych elms, which are com- moner in Wales, appeared to be more resistant, but many of these have now also succumbed. Similar losses of elms have occurred in mainland Europe and North America. Of the various epidemics in Britain, it is thought that the recent and more virulent strain of the disease was brought in on imported **timber**.

The bark beetles only infect elm trees if the trunks are wide enough to let them burrow. It is therefore worth planting elms in the hope that they will be spared and able to grow to maturity. If you have an elm tree which is affected, there is little you can do about it, although natural regeneration from suckers can sometimes occur. Methods of injecting various "antidotes" do exist, but they are seldom effective. Dead elm trees can drop branches without warning and blow over in gales, so fell any that are near your house.

Earthworms a group of segmented, **soil**-living worms, all of which play an invaluable role in creating a good **soil structure**. They take in **organic matter** and soil, which they combine and deposit as **wormcasts**, and their burrows provide good aeration and **drainage**.

Earwig an insect that is easy to recognize by its prominent rear pincers. Earwigs are commonly thought of as harmful, but they are in fact good **natural predators**, eating a variety of **pests**, including small **caterpillars**, **aphids**, and **codling moth** eggs. The damage that they do – mainly nibbling at **fruit** and **flowers** – is relatively minor. Earwigs feed at night and find narrow crevices to hide in by day. Unfortunately, the densely petalled flowers of dahlias and chrysanthemums make ideal resting places and if you are growing these for cutting, earwigs can become quite a pest. Catch them by providing an alternative shelter, such as a traditional **trap** made from a flowerpot stuffed with **straw**, and release them well away from your flowers.

EBDCs abbreviated name for the group of ethylenebis-dithiocarbamate **fungicides**, which includes **maneb**, **mancozeb**, and **zineb**; any of these may contain **ethylene thiourea** as a contaminant, **degradation product**, or **metabolite**.

Eco-friendly currently popular labelling term, supposed to identify consumer products whose manufacture or use causes little or no damage to the environment, although there is as yet no legislation regulating use of the term.

Some of these products are genuinely better for the environment, but others are simply labelled eco-friendly as part of manufacturers' advertising campaigns. Do not therefore automatically believe a label that proclaims something as environmentally safe. Instead, read the small print carefully and check up on the individual ingredients listed.

Ecology the interactive relationships that exist between plants and animals and their surroundings.

To practise **organic gardening** successfully, you will need to have a thorough knowledge of the ecology of the garden, including an understanding of the complex life cycles and the varying needs and functions of the different role players – the pollinators, **natural predators**, and **parasites**, to name but a few.

Eelworms microscopic soil **pests**, also known as nematodes. There are many different species. The stem eelworm can damage many **vegetable** crops, ornamentals, and **strawberries**. It is a **parasite**, feeding inside the plant, and causes a range of symptoms including stunting and distortion. You can prevent stem eelworm problems by **rotation** of crops, and by buying plants from a reputable source or by raising them yourself.

The potato cyst eelworm (sometimes called the golden nematode) is a serious **potato** pest, stunting growth and reducing yields. If you examine potato roots in mid summer, you may see the small brown or white pinhead cysts. As well as rotating crops and buying certified seed tubers, you can reduce damage by growing early **varieties** which will be more mature by the time the eelworm attacks. There are a few **resistant varieties** of potato. However, those that are resistant to one strain of cyst eelworm, but still susceptible to others, are of limited use.

Egg shells a rich source of **calcium**, which you can put on the **compost heap** for **recycling** back into the **soil**. You can also try using a **barrier** of washed and crushed egg shells around young plants to deter **slugs**. These may work in dry conditions, for example, under **cloches**, but rain will soon reduce their effectiveness.

65

Elder a quick-growing **shrub**, native to Britain, of which the common species, *Sambucus nigra*, has clusters of scented white flowers in summer, followed by black berries in autumn. Elder will grow well on most **soil** in an open position. It tends to grow large and straggly, although there are smaller, more compact garden **varieties**. Many insects visit the flowers, while the berries have herbal properties and are loved by the **birds**.

Electric fence electrified wire used for **fencing**. If you have a large garden or smallholding and are thinking of keeping pigs or sheep, an electric fence is a good way of confining them. A few strands of electrified wire do not use up much electricity and are easy to move, and you can cut back further on **energy** costs by using **wind generation** or solar-electric cells to power the fence. You can also buy special electric fences for keeping **rabbits** and foxes out of the garden, and for keeping chickens in.

Elm a common deciduous tree, of the genus *Ulmus*, now sadly depleted as a result of **Dutch Elm Disease**.

Encarsia formosa a small **parasitic wasp** that parasitizes **whitefly** larvae. It is available as a **biological control** which you can introduce into your **greenhouse**. The wasp works by laying its eggs on the whitefly larvae, which appear as white scales on the underside of an infested plant's leaves. The eggs develop and hatch, killing the larvae and producing more wasps to carry on the work. They will only attack whitefly, so there is no risk to humans or any other creatures. *Encarsia* is usually sold through the post in the form of parasitized whitefly larvae attached to cards, which you can hang in the greenhouse. Introduce the larvae as soon as possible after you first see the **pests** in spring, rather than letting numbers build up.

Endive see **Lettuce**.

Energy available energy resources. Access to vast amounts of solar energy, stored in the form of fossil fuels – coal, oil, and natural gas – powered the emergence of modern industrial society. Today, the burning of these fuels is known to contribute to **acid rain**, **air pollution**, and **global warming**. In addition, natural reserves of both them and the uranium used to create nuclear fission energy are fast being depleted, and will eventually run out. Public awareness of these factors has led to increased emphasis on renewable resources and energy conservation.

An obvious way of saving energy in the garden is to cut back on, or abandon altogether, the use of motor-powered **machinery**, such as electric hedge cutters and lawn mowers. However, there are other gardening materials and products with hidden energy costs: artificial **fertilizers**, for example, use up a lot of energy in their manufacture, as do other **agrochemicals**. Use **compost** as an alternative to chemical fertilizers. **Plastic** is another material to cut back on, since it takes a great deal of energy to manufacture and needs replacing frequently, being easily degraded by sunlight. Also, whenever possible, consider reusing materials for **fencing** or **compost bins** rather than buying new **timber** or specially made units. See also **Recycling**.

Erosion the wearing-away process that occurs when **soil** is washed away or blown off the surface of the ground. Poor **soil structure**, brought about through over **cultivation** and lack of **organic matter**, may increase vulnerability to erosion, and it is a particular problem on exposed or sloping sites. You can best avoid erosion by keeping the soil covered, either with a growing crop, a **green manure**, or a **mulch**.

Ethylene thiourea (ETU) a contaminant, **degradation product**, and **metabolite** of **EBDC** fungicides, such as **mancozeb**, **maneb**, and **zinc**. The US Environmental Protection Agency classifies this chemical as **oncogenic** and a **teratogen** in animals.

ETU see **Ethylene thiourea**.

Farmyard manure (FYM) usually a mixture of cattle or sheep **manure** and **straw**, traditionally used to restore **soil fertility**. The straw content of FYM will also help to improve **soil structure**. However, you should avoid buying manure from a farm with intensively kept livestock, since it may be contaminated with antibiotics and metals, such as copper and **zinc**. Organically run or deep-litter cattle farms are preferable sources.

Either dig FYM into the soil or spread it as a **mulch**. Be careful not to put fresh manure too near to plants since it may scorch their leaves. If you have time and space, it is best to **compost** manure before use (see **Manure** for details). This will prevent **leaching** (a particular risk during winter when there are fewer growing plants to take up **nutrients**) and give any **agrochemicals** that may be present more time to break down into harmless by-products.

Fenarimol a **systemic fungicide**, used both for prevention and cure of **mildew** on **fruit** and roses. Fenarimol has a **harvest interval** of 14 days and can cause damage to **trees**; it is dangerous to fish. Try **cultural control** instead.

Fencing an effective means of preventing garden plants from being trampled on or eaten by marauding animals. Slatted fencing is preferable to a solid structure since it serves as an effective **windbreak**, without creating damaging eddies or stagnant conditions, and also provides an ideal support for **climbers**. However, **hedges** are almost always better than fences because they not only act as windbreaks but also, if you choose the right species, provide food plants and **habitats** for wildlife as well. However, they do take time to grow so you may need to install fencing, even if only as a temporary measure.

When buying fencing **timber**, you need to consider its durability, the source from which it has come, and the way it has been treated. If possible, purchase timber from a sustainable source and choose British-grown species with durable heartwood, such as oak, sweet chestnut, larch, and Douglas fir, which are relatively resistant to rotting. Alternatively, consider reusing timber, if you can get hold of a sufficient quantity (see **Recycling**). Since the outer sapwood of all trees grown in the UK rots after a few years without treatment, you will probably need to use some type of **timber treatment**.

Fenitrothion an **insecticide** of the **organophosphorus** group, used against a wide range of **pests**. It is a poison, which may be absorbed through the skin, an **anticholinesterase** substance, and a potential **mutagen**. Fenitrothion is harmful to pets and wildlife, including **bees** and fish, and research in the USA found that **bird** populations were reduced after spraying of minimal amounts of this chemical. It has a **harvest interval** of one to two weeks. Try **cultural control**, **biological control**, **traps**, and **barriers** instead. Only resort to **natural insecticides**, such as **derris**, if all else fails.

Fenarimol
Fencing
Fenitrothion

68

Fenugreek an annual **green manure** and a **legume**, *Trigonella foenum-graecum*. It will fix **nitrogen** but only if the necessary **bacteria** are present in the **soil**. Dig it in after two to three months in spring and summer. It is hardy enough to stand a mild winter (see **Green manures** chart. pp. 80-1).

Ferrous sulphate a **herbicide**, used to control **moss** on turf. It is moderately toxic if swallowed and research suggests that it may be a **mutagen**. It is also toxic to aquatic life, even at low concentrations. See **Lawn maintenance** for safer, alternative methods of moss control.

Fertilizers, artificial chemical compounds used to replace **nutrients** and restore **soil fertility**. Most are sold in powder or granular form and either applied directly or in solution; others are available as **liquid feeds**. The principle ones contain **nitrates** and **phosphates**.

Artificial fertilizers are environmentally unsound for several reasons. Firstly, finite natural resources are used in their manufacture and, in the case of nitrate especially, valuable **energy** reserves. Secondly, **leaching** of excess nitrates causes serious water **pollution** and can also lead to the build up of potentially harmful **residues** in food crops. Thirdly, some nitrate may be released as nitrogen oxide, an air pollutant and contributor to **acid rain** and **global warming**. Artificial fertilizers are in any case unacceptable in **organic gardening** because they act too quickly – feeding plants directly rather than the **soil**. This upsets the balance of soil life, causing some **microorganisms** to disappear and the quality of the soil to deteriorate gradually. They also fail to provide the balanced supply of nutrients and **trace elements** which plants need to grow properly and stay healthy, and while they may promote rapid growth, resultant crops commonly have a higher water content, lower **nutrient** quality, and are more liable to succumb to **pests** and **disease**. See **Natural fertilizers** for safer, alternative methods of feeding the soil.

Fertilizers, natural see **Natural fertilizers**.

Field beans an agricultural variety of broad **bean**, *Vicia fabia*, used as a winter **green manure**. Sow it in autumn and dig it in in spring, before it flowers (see **Green manures** chart, pp. 80-1). It is a **legume** and will fix **nitrogen**.

Fenugreek
Ferrous sulphate
Fertilizers, artificial
Fertilizers, natural
Field beans

Field maple a woodland **tree**, *Acer campestre*, native to Britain, which you can grow as part of a mixed garden **hedge**. It has colourful autumn foliage and winged fruits which are popular with **birds**. It will grow well in the majority of garden **soils**.

Fireblight a serious **disease** which mainly affects **pears**, **apples**, **hawthorn**, **cotoneaster**, **pyracantha**, and some other **trees** of the Rosaceae family. Symptoms include dark brown leaves (which appear scorched), brown, wrinkled fruits, and reddish brown tissue beneath the bark. Mature trees can die in six months. Root up and burn any that are affected. Avoid planting host plants in areas where the disease is a problem.

Field maple
Fireblight
Fish meal
Flameweeding

Fish meal a rich top-up source of **nitrogen** and **phosphorus**. It is acceptable in **organic gardening** because it uses a **waste** product, but you should not need to use it if you are making your own **compost** and using **rotation** and **green manures** effectively. Also, some brands contain chemical **potassium**, so if you do decide to use it, read the small print carefully to ensure that you are buying an unadulterated product. Fish meal is obviously unsuitable for **vegan gardening**.

Flameweeding a method of **weed control** that uses a flame-weeder, or flame gun. This device produces enough heat to kill **weeds** by bursting the plants' cells. There is no need actually to scorch the foliage. Flameweeding is a good method of keeping down weeds on **paths**, and you can also use it on ornamental and **vegetable** beds around plants with tough stems. A technique frequently employed by commercial growers is to flame a seedbed just before a crop emerges to kill weed seedlings, but you have to time this just right for it to be effective!

Flameweeders are fuelled by gas or paraffin, the gas models generally being easier to use. They consume a great deal of **energy** and are therefore not recommended for use where hand **weeding**, **hoeing**, or alternative methods of **clearing ground** are possible. They are also potentially dangerous so you should use them with great care, following manufacturer's instructions closely and not employing them when children or pets are around. As a precaution, you should also make sure that they are stored well out of the reach of children.

Fleabeetle a small, dark, shiny beetle, which is a **pest** of **brassicas** and some other plants. Fleabeetles eat away small holes in the leaves of seedlings, frequently causing severe damage. They are especially active in hot, dry weather when you often see them jumping near affected plants. You can prevent attacks by placing a protective **fleece** over the plants. Alternatively, reduce the likelihood of damage by encouraging seedlings to grow strongly, ensuring, in particular, that they have plenty of water. Raise plants in a **greenhouse**, if necessary. Since beetles will jump up if plants are disturbed, you can trap them by holding a sticky board in one hand and rustling infested leaves with the other. As a last resort, dust young plants with the **natural insecticide, derris**.

Fleabeetle
Fleece
Flowers
Formothion

Fleece a lightweight material, usually made from spun polypropylene, used for covering crops. Fleeces were originally designed for **frost** protection, but they are also good for keeping off small, flying **pests**, such as **aphids** and **carrot fly**. You can remove fleece when a crop has passed the vulnerable stage in its growth or leave it in place on low-growing crops which are relatively quick to mature, such as **lettuce**, **carrots**, and **Chinese cabbage**. The material is so light that it can ride on top of plants without harming them or restricting their growth. For that reason, it is sometimes called a "floating mulch". Handle fleece with care, and it should last several seasons.

Flowers plants grown principally for their ornamental blossom. Flowers are as much part of **organic gardening** as **fruit** and **vegetable** crops. They add **diversity** and many are good **attractant plants**, providing nectar and pollen for **beneficial insects**, which are the natural enemies of garden **pests**. Most flowers are not difficult to grow without using chemicals, provided that you give them the right conditions. Never put sun-loving plants in the shade or moisture-loving plants in dry **soil** because plants given the wrong conditions will never thrive and will be more susceptible to pests and **diseases**. Look out for **resistant varieties** of flowers: certain antirrhinums show resistance to **rust**, for example.

Formothion a **systemic insecticide** of the **organophosphorus** group, used against a wide range of **pests**. It is a poison

71

and research on bacterial cultures suggests that it is a **mutagen**. It is toxic to **bees**, slightly poisonous to fish, and has moderate **persistence**. Try **cultural control**, **biological control**, **traps**, and **barriers** instead. Only use **natural insecticides**, such as **derris**, as a last resort.

French beans see **Beans**.

French beans
Frog
Froghopper
Frost

Frog an amphibian and a **natural predator** of garden **pests**, including large numbers of small **slugs**. Frogs need damp conditions in which to live and will happily take up residence in your garden if there is a patch of long, damp vegetation. However, they require water, ideally a **pond**, in which to breed, and a sloping edge or wooden plank to help them get out on to dry land. Adding a little frog spawn to a pond is a good way of starting a colony, but it is best to check with your local Wildlife Trust (see Useful Addresses, pp. 190-1) before taking any from the wild. Avoid the use of **slug** pellets which are poisonous to frogs, as are slugs that have been poisoned by them.

Froghopper a small, jumping, insect, which is a garden **pest** and the cause of the white, frothy blobs of "cuckoo spit" that you see on plants. Inside each protective blob is a froghopper nymph feeding on the plant sap. They usually appear on ornamental or wild plants, and also on cultivated **raspberries** and **blackberries**. The damage to the plant is minimal, and you can remove the froth and nymphs easily with a jet of water.

Frost a fall in temperature below freezing, which can affect plants if they are not sufficiently hardy. The area your garden is in, together with its altitude and distance from the coast, will determine the frequency and severity of frost. However, local conditions have an influence: cities are usually warmer than rural areas, and valley bottoms are frost prone because cold air settles there. Avoid putting solid **fencing** and **walls** across a slope because they can stop the flow of cold air and create a frost pocket. You can protect tender plants from frost by using **cloches** or **fleeces**. During critical periods, keep the **soil** around them free from **weeds** and light-coloured **mulches** since bare soil helps raise the temperature, absorbing heat during the day and releasing it at night.

You can protect the blossom of fruit trees in spring with an **irrigation** system, positioned so that it will cover the bloom with a fine spray of water whenever frost threatens. Wind makes frosts more penetrating, so **windbreaks** can also give protection.

Fruit any type of **tree**, **bush**, or **cane fruit**. You can grow all kinds of fruit organically, even in a small garden. For example, train fruit trees on **walls** and **fencing**, or grow them on "dwarfing" **rootstocks** to restrict their size.

It is important to choose fruit which suits your site. Most needs sunshine and some shelter, but certain types are more tolerant than others. Where spring **frosts** are likely to damage blossom, look for late-flowering **varieties**. Try local fruit tree varieties since sometimes these will do best, and you will be helping to keep them in cultivation.

The ideal **soil** for fruit is deep, well-drained, and slightly acid. **Soil testing** before planting will enable you to correct any **soil deficiencies**. You should also dig in well-rotted **manure** or **compost**. Too much feeding can result in leafy growth at the expense of fruit, but regularly applying **mulches** of **organic matter** around trees and bushes will usually supply sufficient **nutrients**. Most fruit varieties are now available from **virus-free stock**, and it is well worth looking for this guarantee. There are also many modern varieties that have been bred with resistance to specific **diseases** (see **Resistant varieties**).

Fruit cage a netted framework used to protect **bush** and **cane fruit** from **birds**. The cage can have permanent netting on the sides, but ideally it should have a removable netted top, which you can take off at the end of the season to allow the **birds** to feed on overwintering **pests** and any remaining fruit.

Fumigant a form of **pesticide**, released as a poisonous gas or smoke, usually by setting light to a cone, pellet, or powder, used in **greenhouses** and other confined spaces. They are among the most dangerous of pesticides, posing health risks to humans through leakage, and capable of killing a wide range of invertebrates, including useful **natural predators**. Replace with **cultural control**, **biological control**, **traps**, and **barriers**, only using **natural insecticides**, such as **derris**, if all else fails.

Fruit
Fruit cage
Fumigant

Fungi spore-bearing plants that are either **parasites** or saprophytes (the latter live off dead material). Fungi, such as puffballs and mushrooms, sometimes appear on **lawns** and do little harm. Some parasitic species, known as mycorrhizal fungi, have **symbiotic** relationships with many plants, including **trees**, in which they supply valuable **nutrients** from the **soil** which the host plant cannot collect for itself. However, a few fungi, for example, moulds, **mildews** and **rusts**, cause **disease** in **fruit**, **vegetables**, and ornamental plants. See also **Honey fungus**.

Fungicide any **pesticide** used against **fungi**. Unfortunately many fungicides harm beneficial fungi and other creatures, including useful **natural predators**, and some, such as **benomyl** and **captan**, can seriously endanger human health. Although their potential for destroying mycorrhizal fungi has never been properly quantified, this may be an important factor in the reduced growth rate of certain treated crops. Try **cultural control** instead. Only resort to the **copper fungicide**, **Bordeaux mixture**, if all other measures fail.

Furniture, garden a useful addition to the garden if made from durable material and built to withstand adverse weather conditions. Whether making your own or buying ready-made wooden benches, tables, or chairs, it is important to ascertain the type of **timber** used, its source, and whether or not it has been pretreated. An increasing proportion of garden furniture is made from **tropical hardwoods**, which are being felled far more quickly than they are replaced, and exported and sold at cheap rates. If you can, buy from sources which guarantee that the timber comes from a sustainably managed source. Also check that the wood is sufficiently hard wearing for the use envisaged and avoid any that has been pretreated with toxic **wood preservatives**, such as **creosote**, **gamma HCH** and **pentachlorphenol**. See **Timber treatment** for safer, alternative methods of preserving wood.

Gaia the concept of the planet as a self-regulating, living entity, formulated by the scientist, James Lovelock. Under this hypothesis, a complicated series of feedback mechanisms exist that maintain conditions suitable for life on the planet. This system can sustain a certain amount of damage, for example, in the form of **pollution**, but threatened major crises, such as **global warming**, have the potential to upset the feedback mechanisms and to create new conditions – not necessarily beneficial to humans.

Gall a growth on a plant created after stimulation by **fungi**, **bacteria**, or a parasitic insect (as a source of shelter and food for its larvae). Examples include oak apples, which are not really **apples** at all, but tumours produced on **oak** leaves by a **parasitic wasp**. Most galls are created by a female insect injecting her eggs inside the plant, along with a chemical to stimulate the gall to develop. The larvae live inside the gall, protected from **natural predators** and adverse weather, and feed freely on the host plant. In the case of the oak apple, several other species have also adapted to lay their eggs inside the gall, thereby parasitizing a **parasite**. Galls do little harm unless a plant is heavily infested, although they can be hard to distinguish from more harmful forms of **canker** or **disease**.

Gamma HCH an **organochlorine insecticide**, used either alone or in mixtures against **pests** and for seed treatment; otherwise known as lindane. Gamma HCH is also employed as a **wood preservative**. This is one of the most hazardous **pesticides** available for garden use. It is highly poisonous if swallowed, inhaled, or absorbed through the skin, and has a range of adverse health effects, including damage to the central nervous system. Evidence that it is a **carcinogen** exists and it is a suspected **teratogen**. Gamma HCH is **persistent**, with a **harvest interval** of one to two weeks. It is extremely toxic to all wildlife, including **bees**, and its use as a preservative on roofing timbers is thought to be a major cause of the decline in **bat** populations in Britain – treated wood can remain toxic to bats for up to 20 years. Many plants are damaged by its use, including **carrots**, **potatoes**, and soft **fruit**. Use of Gamma HCH has been either banned or restricted in many countries, including Argentina, Canada, Germany, Finland, New Zealand, and the USSR. Use untreated seeds and safer, alternative methods of containing pests, including **cultural control**, **biological control**, **traps**, and **barriers**. Only resort to **natural insecticides**, such as **derris**, if all else fails. For details on safer methods of treating wood, see **Timber treatment**.

Garlic
Genetic
conservation

Garlic see **Onions**.

Genetic conservation the practice of preserving genetic diversity in plants through the conservation of different **varieties**. At the present time, we are losing irreplaceable genetic plant material as many rare species and varieties become extinct. Even on a garden scale, literally thousands of traditional varieties of **vegetables** and **fruit** are disappearing from circulation.

In the case of vegetables, this is partly due to plant-patenting legislation, which has made it illegal to sell any seeds or **potato** tubers that are not registered on an official "National List". The high cost to manufacturers of keeping individual varieties on the list has meant that many traditional, less commercially viable varieties have been abandoned. Many of these had qualities of particular interest to the organic gardener, such as disease resistance or adaptations to local conditions.

No such legislation of this type governs fruit, but commercial advertising has put growers under pressure to produce "popular" varieties. In Britain, for example, where we used to have over 400 varieties of **apple**, each with its distinctive taste, we now sell less than a dozen. Today's varieties are chosen for looks rather than quality and for their ability to withstand mechanized harvesting and packaging and lengthy transport and storage periods.

Many traditional garden **flowers** are also being lost through commercial pressures on consumers to buy short-term bedding plants, not necessarily adapted to local conditions and frequently vulnerable to **pest** and **disease** attack. In addition, the habitats of dozens of wild plant species are now under threat from development and accompanying industrial pollution (see **Lichens** and **Moss**).

In the UK, efforts to counteract these trends include the vegetable gene bank at the Horticultural Research International at Wellesbourne, and, for amateur gardeners, the seed library at the Henry Doubleday Research Association (see Useful Addresses, pp. 190-1). HDRA encourages gardeners to try and keep old strains alive by swapping seeds and cultivating traditional fruit and vegetables. With regard to ornamental plants, much of the conservation effort in this area is coordinated by The National Council for the Conservation of Plants and Gardens (see Useful Addresses, pp. 190-1).

Global warming
Glyphosate

Global warming the theory that the planet is gradually warming up, due to an increased amount of the sun's heat being trapped in the atmosphere by pollutant gases; also known as the greenhouse effect. Some of the gases are the result of environmentally unsound industrial and agricultural practices: carbon dioxide, in particular, but also **methane** and nitrogen oxide, are released by the burning of fossil fuels and wood. These "greenhouse gases" increase the proportion of the sun's energy retained in the atmosphere by re-reflecting some of the solar energy which has bounced off the planet's surface, in the same way that a **greenhouse** does. Global warming is not proven yet, but most of the world's climatologists are now convinced that it is occurring. If so, it will affect us all. Weather patterns will become more unstable and as, some of the ice caps melt, sea levels will rise. You can do your bit to prevent global warming by not having **bonfires** and by taking steps to reduce **energy** use.

Glyphosate a **translocated herbicide** used for general **weed control**. There are considerable risks associated with **spray**

drift of this chemical, except in cases where it is used for **spot treatment**. Use hand **weeding**, **hoeing**, forking, or apply a **mulch** for **clearing ground**.

Goldenrod perennial plants of the genus *Solidago*. There are summer- and late-flowering varieties, all of which are good **attractant plants**, and also popular with **bees**. Most are tall with yellow flowers. They grow easily on any sunny or lightly shaded site.

Gooseberries see **Bush fruit**.

Gooseberry sawfly see **Sawfly**.

Grass mowings see **Lawn mowings**.

Grazing rye an annual **green manure**, *Secale cereale*, with an extensive root system, invaluable for improving **soil struc-ture**. It grows fast, providing good **ground cover**, and is one of the best green manures for suppressing **weeds**. Sow it in late autumn, after summer crops have been cleared, and dig it in in spring before it begins to get tough (see **Green manures** chart, pp. 80-1). It is a cereal, unrelated to any **vegetables**, so use it anywhere in your **rotation**.

Greasebands bands of **vegetable** grease placed around, or painted on, the trunks of **apple**, **pear**, and **plum trees** as a control against the **winter moth**. They prevent this common **pest** from crawling up the trunks. You can either buy greased paper strips to tie on, or purchase the special grease and paint it on. Do not use ordinary engine grease. Also, do not paint directly on to the bark of young trees since this can damage them. Position the bands about 30cm (12in) above **soil** level, both on the trunk and on the tree stake if there is one.

Greenfly see **Aphids**.

Greenhouse a glass- or plastic-covered structure, either free-standing or lean-to, which is designed to trap solar radiation and to protect plants from the wind, thus extending the length of the growing season and facilitating **plant raising**. Under greenhouse cover you can grow a wide range of plants, including tender food crops, such as **toma-**

toes and **peppers**, and a variety of exotic species. You can opt for a preconstructed greenhouse or build your own from a DIY kit. Alternatively, make a polytunnel from pliable poles – bent into half circles to form hoops and erected in a line – and a **plastic** covering. Choose the type of plastic that is meant for this use, or it will quickly crack and break up in the sun.

If you want to grow throughout the year, your greenhouse will need heating, which can be costly to install and run. However, you can minimize on expenditure and conserve **energy** generally by designing a **solar greenhouse** with a passive **solar heating** system.

Greenhouses, unfortunately, provide ideal living conditions for many **pests**, including **slugs** and **snails**. Also, some greenhouse-grown **vegetables** can build up quite high **nitrate** levels during the winter months, something you may wish to avoid.

Greenhouse effect see **Global warming**.

Green manures crops cultivated, not for consumption, but to improve both the **nutrient** content of the **soil** and the **soil structure**. As they grow, green manures take up and store nutrients that might otherwise be washed away. They also protect the soil surface from extremes of temperature and heavy rain, and help prevent **weed** growth. When a green manure reaches a certain stage (see chart pp. 80-1), you should return it to the soil by **digging** or **rotavating**, or by cutting it and leaving it on the soil surface as a **mulch** for the **earthworms** to take under. It will provide valuable **organic matter** and gradually release stored nutrients.

Certain green manures, such as **alfalfa**, have deep roots which can break up heavy soils. Others have masses of fine roots which greatly help the soil structure, for example, **grazing rye**. Those which are **legumes**, for instance **tares**, take valuable **nitrogen** from the air and fix it in the soil, provided the correct **bacteria** are present. They are sometimes sown underneath other crops to provide them with nitrogen and to control weeds.

When choosing a green manure, consider the time of year you want to sow it, how long it is to be in ground, and how it will fit into your crop **rotation** (see chart). After digging in a green manure, wait about three or four weeks before putting in a subsequent crop.

Grey mould see **Botrytis**.

Ground beetle a dark beetle (see p. 16), many species of
which are good **natural predators**. They eat **slugs**, **root aphids**,
the larvae of **cabbage** and **carrot root flies** and other **pests**,
feeding mainly at night. During the day they appreciate
plenty of shelter. Encourage them by laying down thick
mulches or growing **ground cover plants**.

You can use ground beetles to help protect a patch of
young plants from slugs. Surround the plot with a shallow

Grey mould
Ground beetle
**Green manures
(chart)**

How to use green manures

Crop	Life cycle	Sowing times
Alfalfa *Medicago sativa*	Perennial	April to July
Buckwheat *Fagopyrum esculentum*	Annual	Middle of March to August
+**Clover, crimson** *Trifolium incarnatum*	Annual	March to August
Clover, Essex red *Trifolium pratense*	Perennial	April to August
+**Fenugreek** *Trigonella foenum-graecum*	Annual	March to August
Field beans *Vicia fibia*	Annual	September to November
Grazing rye *Secale cereale*	Annual	Mid August to November
Lupin, bitter *Lupinus angustifolius*	Annual	March to June
+**Mustard** *Sinapis alba*	Annual	March to mid September
+**Phacelia** *Phacelia tanacetifolia*	Annual	End of March to mid September
Tares *Vicia sativa*	Annual	March to mid September
Trefoil *Medicago lupulina*	Annual/Biennial	Mid March to mid August

+Makes useful growth if autumn sown but may be hit by a hard frost.

pitfall **trap** made, for example, from metal lawn edging. Some ground beetles are bound to fall over the edge into the trap and, being unable to climb out, will seek out all the slugs in this confined area. Always put a few flat stones within the trap for the beetles to shelter under.

Ground cover plants dense, low-growing perennial plants used to cover and protect the **soil** and to fill the space between taller plants and **shrubs**. Heathers and ivy are good examples. Plant them in ground that is free from

Ground cover plants

Sowing rate	Time in ground	Plot in crop rotation
2 to 3g per sq m (7.6 sq ft)	From 3 months	Legume
10g per sq m (7.6 sq ft)	2 to 3 months	Any
2 to 3g per sq m (7.6 sq ft)	2 to 3 months in summer	Legume
1.5 to 3g per sq m (7.6 sq ft)	3 months to 2 years	Legume
5g per sq m (7.6 sq ft)	2 to 3 months in summer	Legume
10cm (4in) apart in rows 4.5 to 6m (15 to 20ft) apart	About 5 months over winter	Legume
30g per sq m (7.6 sq ft)	Over winter	Any
5 to 10cm (2 to 4 in) apart in rows 20 cm (8in) apart	2 to 3 months	Legume
3 to 5g per sq m (7.6 sq ft)	3 to 8 weeks in summer	Brassica
2 to 3g per sq m (7.6 sq ft)	Up to 2 months in summer	Any
20g per sq m (7.6 sq ft)	2 to 3 months in summer, or over winter	Legume
1.5 to 3g per sq m (7.6 sq ft)	3 months to 1 year	Legume

perennial **weeds**, and keep the area clear until they are established. Once they have formed a dense mat, they will suppress most weed growth.

Growbags commercially available, heavy-duty **plastic** bags filled with a **potting-compost** mixture. These are used for growing crops where you do not have the space to plant them directly in the **soil**, or where growing conditions are not suitable. They are useful if you only have a back yard or balcony, or in a **greenhouse** if you want to avoid planting in infected **soil**. Try growing two consecutive crops in the same growbag – start with a demanding one, for example, **tomatoes**, and then follow this with one which needs less **nutrients**, such as **lettuce**.

Most growbags on the market contain **peat** (which you should avoid since the cutting of it causes serious environmental damage) and artificial **fertilizers**. If you cannot find one containing an organic mixture, you can make your own (see **Potting compost** recipes). It is not easy to give plants in growbags enough water or a balanced supply of nutrients, so only use them if you have no available ground in the garden.

Growbags
Guelder rose
Gypsum

Guelder rose a **shrub**, *Viburnum opulus*, native to Britain, which you can also grow in a mixed garden **hedge**. It has colourful autumn foliage and red berries, loved by **birds**. It will grow well in most garden **soils**, but prefers moisture.

Gypsum a natural form of calcium sulphate, which you can use in the garden as a means of countering shortages of **sulphur** or **calcium**, without altering **pH**. You can also use it for **soil** improvement on heavy clay. In Britain, some gypsum is mined from sensitive areas, such as the Derbyshire and Yorkshire National Parks.

Habitat the natural home of a plant or animal, inclusive of all factors that affect its survival, such as geography, **climate**, food, **natural predators**, and **soil type**. Some species have very specialized habitats while others are tolerant of a wide range of conditions. In order to provide habitats for a variety of plants and wildlife, you should aim to increase **diversity** in your garden.

Hair clippings the cut hair of humans and animals, a valuable source of **nitrogen** which you can add to the **compost heap**. It decomposes slowly so add enough to make up 1-2% of the heap, but not more.

Halo blight a bacterial **disease** that affects French and runner **beans**, causing dark, moist spots on leaves; these later darken and dry out and appear surrounded by yellowish "halos". In severe attacks, plants can become stunted and seedlings may die. The disease is mainly seed borne, but can be spread by rain. Remove and destroy infected plants, and never collect seed from them. Do not soak bean seeds in water before sowing them since this can spread the **bacteria**. Instead, pregerminate them in damp **leafmould**. Use **resistant varieties** if this disease is a problem.

Handpicking a method of physically removing **pests** by hand. Where only a few plants are infested, this can be an effective method of control: you can easily pick off **cater-**

pillars and **sawfly** larvae, for example. Keep a close watch on plants and catch pests before they spread. Learn to spot their eggs and rub them off before they hatch.

Hardiness the extent of a plant's ability to withstand adverse weather conditions in a particular region. If a plant is classified as hardy, this usually means that you can grow it outside all year round. In contrast, a half-hardy plant is one that cannot withstand any **frost**, and you should therefore only grow it outside without protection during the summer. Hardiness can depend on the ability of a plant to withstand not only low temperatures but also cold winds and other adverse conditions, and it is an important factor to consider when choosing plants that you hope will flourish on a particular site.

Hare a medium-sized herbivore which usually lives on open grassland. Hares have declined in number in the last few years due to both **habitat** destruction and the harmful effects of the use of certain **pesticides**. **Paraquat**, for example, may harm hares. If they stray on to your land, do not harm them, but if they start eating your **vegetables** or **flowers**, you should put up **fencing** to keep them out. Unlike **rabbits**, they do not usually burrow under fencing, but they can jump higher.

Harvest interval a term written on **pesticide** labels to indicate the time lapse that should be observed between applying a chemical, and harvesting and eating a crop. It is a rough indication of the **persistence** of a chemical. Observing the harvest interval, however, will not guarantee a plant that is free from contamination, since pesticide regulations are set on the assumption that a "safe" level of a chemical, known as the Acceptable Daily Intake, or ADI, can remain on a plant. Only those pesticides that are potentially dangerous if eaten are given a harvest interval, so be wary of **spray drift** on to food crops.

Hawthorn a thorny hedgerow **tree** of the genus *Crataegus*, which is native to Britain. You can grow it as a specimen in a large garden or clip it to form part of a neat garden **hedge**. It has attractive spring blossom and red autumn fruit, or haws, which are loved by **birds**. It will grow well in any garden **soil**, either in sun or partial shade.

84

Hay cut and dried grass, useful for winter feeding of domestic livestock, **rabbits**, and other herbivores. You can grow your own hay by leaving grass to grow and only cutting it once or twice in a season. Meadow flowers growing among the grass will make it more nutritious. To dry hay, leave it spread out on the ground in the sun and turn it occasionally. In damp weather, hang it over a wire fence. Hay makes a good **mulch** in the garden, particularly around **tree** and **bush fruit**. It will break down slowly over the growing season and provide useful **nutrients**.

Hazel a small, deciduous **tree**, *Corylus avellana*, native to Britain, with an attractive display of catkins in late winter or early spring, and nuts in autumn. A single specimen takes up little space, or you can plant several and cut one back each year for **pea** sticks. You can also plant hazel as part as a mixed **hedge**.

Hedge a multi-functional element in any garden. Hedges contribute to the underlying structural framework and can act as effective **windbreaks**, when required. Hedges also provide privacy for humans, and are good places for **birds** to shelter and nest. However, you must allow for the fact that hedges create shade, and compete with other plants for water and **nutrients**.

There are many different hedging plants to choose from. In Britain, one of the best hedges for an organic garden would consist of a mixture of **native plants** such as **hawthorn**, **buckthorn**, **guelder rose**, **holly**, and **field maple**. You can clip these into a neat and attractive formal hedge or, if you have the space, leave them to grow more naturally so that they provide extra berries and seeds for birds. Informal flowering hedges, such as lavender, look attractive and are also loved by **bees**. Prickly hedges of **berberis** or holly are useful for keeping out unwanted animals.

For both shelter and wildlife, a mixture of evergreen and deciduous plants is probably best. Coniferous and evergreen hedges are often too dense to make efficient windbreaks, and although they do provide good cover for wildlife, they usually supply little food. A deciduous hedge, on the other hand, can be too open in winter.

Hedgehog a small, spiny-backed mammal, with a hearty appetite for **slugs** and **snails**. In Britain, hedgehog populations are sadly declining. Those you see flattened on the road represent only some of the casualties; many others die because their **habitats** are destroyed or from poisoning.

You can encourage and keep hedgehogs in your garden in several ways. First and foremost, avoid use of slug pellets since these can kill hedgehogs, as can the bodies of slugs that have been poisoned by the pellets. Secondly, leave an area of wild, dense, shrubby vegetation for the hedgehog to live in, if there is no rough scrub nearby. Thirdly, you can build a hedgehog box for the animal to live or nest in, 50 x 40 x 40cm (20 x 16 x 16in), and attach a narrow entrance tunnel, 10cm (4in) sq and 30cm (12in) long. Avoid feeding hedgehogs milk or buns since this cuts down on the number of **pests** they eat, and is not a particularly good staple diet for the young ones.

Heptenophos a **systemic insecticide** of the **organophosphorus** group, used to control **aphids** on **fruit**, **vegetables**, and pot plants under glass. It is a poison and **anticholinesterase** compound, with a **harvest interval** of at least a day. Heptenophos is harmful to **bees** and fish.

Herb drier a simple, box-like, solar-powered device, which is designed to speed up the drying of **herbs** for winter use. It consists of a vertical box with holes in the lid, which is positioned over a simple solar panel. Herbs are stacked in the box, so that hot air rises up through the herbs before passing out of air holes at the top. This speeds up the drying and also protects herbs from direct sunlight, which can destroy some of their flavour.

Herbicide any **pesticide** that is used to kill unwanted plants, or **weeds**; also known as a weedkiller. There are hundreds of different herbicides available. They may work selectively, targeting grasses or broad-leaved plants, or act as general weedkillers, destroying any plant. Some kill on contact, while other **translocated herbicides** enter the plant at one point and travel around the organism, damaging and eventually destroying it. Certain herbicides, such as **paraquat**, are highly toxic to humans and other animals, while almost all can damage plants other than weeds, either through accidental contamination or **spray drift**. For details on safer, alternative methods of controlling unwanted plants, see **Weed control**.

Heptenophos
Herb drier
Herbicide

Herbs plants commonly used for flavouring, in medicine, and in cosmetic preparations. Many herbs also have attractive **flowers** and foliage, and provide nectar or pollen for **beneficial insects** and **bees** and **butterflies**. Those in the plant family Labiatae are all good bee plants, and the **umbellifers** attract **hoverflies**.

The ideal place for a bed of culinary herbs is close to the kitchen door. However, you can plant many of the more decorative herbs in an ornamental border, and annuals and biennials, such as dill and parsley, will fit conveniently into a vegetable **rotation**. Some herbs, such as lavender, make good low-growing **hedges**. Others, such as creeping thyme, flourish in between paving slabs on a **path** or patio. Only the more rampant herbs, or those dug for their roots, for example, horseradish, need a separate bed.

Shrubby, aromatic herbs, for instance, thyme, like a well-drained **soil** that it is not too rich, otherwise they make over-lush growth and have less scent and flavour. Leafy herbs, such as parsley, need more moisture and **nutrients**. Most herbs suffer relatively little from **pests** and **diseases**. See also chart on pp. 88-9.

Herbs
Hoeing
Holly

Hoeing a method of **cultivation**, which uses the hoe – a long-handled **tool** with a fine blade – to till the **soil** and cut **weeds** off from their roots. Hoeing is one of the easiest ways to deal with annual or seedling **weeds**. You can use it to clean an area before planting or as a method of **weed control** between established plants, and also on gravel **paths** and drives. However, hoeing is not effective in wet conditions. Nor does it easily get rid of established perennial weeds, such as dandelions and docks, unless you are persistent (see **Weed control** chart for alternative methods).

Holly one of the few evergreen **trees**, *Ilex aquifolium*, which is native to Britain. It has attractive shiny green leaves and red berries, and provides good winter cover and food for **birds**.

Holly is slow growing and responds well to clipping, making it a good **shrub** or hedging plant even in a small garden. It will grow on most sites provided they are not waterlogged. Male and female flowers are usually borne on separate trees, so you will not necessarily get berries if you only plant one specimen. However, there are cultivated **varieties** which do not present this problem.

How to grow herbs

Herb (plant family)	Life cycle	Growth habit	Flowers attract
Angelica (Umbelliferae)	Biennial/ Perennial	Erect; up to 2 m (6' 6") tall	Hoverflies
Basil (Labiatae)	Usually as an annual	Small, bushy; half hardy	Bees
Bay (Lauraceae)	Perennial	Evergreen shrub/small tree; not very hardy	
Chamomile (Compositae)	Annual/ Perennial	Low growing; creeping perennial varieties	Bees, hoverflies
Chervil (Umbelliferae)	Annual	Delicate, up to 60cm (2') tall; very hardy	Hoverflies
Chives (Liliaceae)	Perennial	Forms compact clumps	Bees
Dill (Umbelliferae)	Annual	Delicate; up to 1m (3' 3") tall	Hoverflies
Fennel (Umbelliferae)	Perennial	Upright, with delicate foliage	Hoverflies
Hyssop (Labiatae)	Perennial	Small, evergreen shrub	Bees
Lavender (Labiatae)	Perennial	Small, evergreen shrub	Bees, butterflies
Lemon balm (Labiatae)	Perennial	Forms bushy clumps	Bees
Marjoram, pot (Labiatae)	Perennial	Bushy, spreading	Bees, butterflies
Mint (Labiatae)	Perennial	Upright bushy growth; has invasive roots	Bees, butterflies
Parsley (Umbelliferae)	Biennial	Low growing, bushy	Not usually left to flower
Rosemary (Labiatae)	Perennial	Small shrub; not completely hardy	Bees
Sage (Labiatae)	Perennial	Small, evergreen shrub	Bees
Savory, winter (Labiatae)	Perennial	Low-growing shrub, usually evergreen	Bees
Tarragon, French (Compositae)	Perennial	Tall, upright growth; needs shelter in cold, wet areas	
Thyme (Labiatae)	Perennial	Bushy, low-growing, and creeping species	Bees

Herb (chart)

Site	Uses/comments
Rich, moist soil; sunny or partially shaded spot	Leaves used for flavouring sweet dishes
Fairly rich soil; sunny, sheltered spot, or grow in a pot in a **greenhouse**	Important cutting herb – best used fresh
Sunny, sheltered spot, or grow in a pot, which you can put inside in winter	Important culinary herb; leaves dry well
Grows in most soils; sunny or lightly shaded spot	Flowers make a soothing tea
Best in rich, moist soil; needs light shade in summer	Mainly a salad herb, best eaten fresh
Best in moist rich soil; sunny site	Leaves used fresh, in salads and garnishings
Fairly rich soil; sunny, sheltered spot	Leaves and seeds have many culinary uses; seeds are also useful medicinally
Fairly rich soil; sunny spot; looks attractive in an ornamental bed	Leaves, stems and seeds have culinary uses; seeds are also useful medicinally
Light, well-drained soil; sunny spot; makes low-growing, flowering hedge	Medicinal uses
As for hyssop	Flowers used for their perfume, and also medicinally
Fairly moist, rich soil; sunny or partially shaded spot	Leaves used to make a refreshing, soothing tea
Light, well-drained soil; sunny position	Culinary and medicinal uses
Rich, moist soil; light shade; contain roots in a bottomless bucket	Leaves have many culinary uses, but can suffer from **rust**
Rich, moist soil; sunny or partially shaded site; makes an attractive edging	Important culinary herb with medicinal properties; **carrot fly** can be a problem
Light, well-drained soil; sunny, sheltered position	Important culinary herb with medicinal properties
Light, well-drained soil; sunny position	Leaves have culinary and medicinal uses
Light, well-drained soil; sunny position; makes a good low-growing hedge	Culinary uses and some medicinal properties
Well drained soil; sunny site	Important culinary herb
Light, well-drained soil; sunny position	Common thyme is the important culinary and medicinal species

Herb (chart)

Honey fungus a serious fungal **disease** of most woody and some herbaceous plants, causing slow decay and death across an area. Toadstools, usually honey yellow in colour, appear in autumn at the base of **trees**, and on sites close to old tree stumps. Affected wood is initially stained under the bark and then becomes white and stringy. You may find bootlace-like strands under the bark and in the surrounding **soil**. **Apple**, birch, cedar, cypress, lilac, pine, privet, walnut, and **willow** are all susceptible.

There is no cure for honey fungus, although you can prevent its spread by **digging** up and burning affected plants and as many of the bootlaces as you can find. Do not replant any woody plants for at least a year in the same plot, and avoid susceptible species.

Honey fungus
Honeysuckle
Hoof and horn meal
Hops
Household scraps

Honeysuckle a twining shrub of which the species *Lonicera periclymenum* is native to Britain. This is one of the best **climbers** for wildlife and well worth growing in the garden. It has scented flowers which attract many insects, particularly moths, and colourful berries that are loved by **birds**.

Its dense mass of stems provide shelter and good nesting places, but they also make it unsuitable for clipping neatly against a **wall**. Honeysuckles prefer a fairly rich, moist **soil** and some shade at their roots. Cultivated garden species and **varieties** may not attract so many insects, but they may flower at different times and some are evergreen.

Hoof and horn meal a **natural fertilizer**, which is a source of slowly released **nitrogen**. Use it on poor **soil** both when planting **fruit** trees and bushes and to boost the growth of leafy crops in spring and summer.

Hops flowers of the hop plant, which are used when dry for brewing beer. You can sometimes buy "spent" hops after they have been used by a brewery. These make a good **mulch** or you can dig them directly into the **soil** to add **organic matter** and a useful quantity of plant **nutrients**.

Household scraps left-over household or **kitchen waste**, which you can separate out and add to the **compost heap**. Any **biodegradable** material is appropriate and good items to include are **fruit** and **vegetable** scraps, **egg shells**, **hair clippings**, and, in small amounts, undyed paper and tea leaves (see **Compost heap** chart, p. 46). Store these in a covered plastic bucket, and empty them regularly on to the compost heap, or on to a pile ready for making into **compost**. Wash the bucket out thoroughly after use.

Household water see **Water resources**.

Hoverflies a family of **beneficial insects** (see p. 16) some species of which resemble small wasps, but with longer, flatter bodies, only a single pair of wings, and no sting. Hoverflies dart from place to place, then hover silently. It is their larvae that eat **aphids** and other small **pests**. You can often spot these pale, flat, legless maggots among aphid colonies. Take care not to squash or spray them.

The adult hoverflies feed on nectar and pollen, and you can encourage them in the garden by growing **attractant plants**. They like most flat, open, single **flowers**, since these are easy for them to work with their short tongues. Particularly attractive to them are the **poached-egg plant**, annual **convolvulus**, pot **marigold**, **buckwheat**, and most **umbellifers**, such as fennel.

Humus a material formed in the **soil** by the breakdown of **organic matter** and from which plant **nutrients** are released. Humus also has the ability to bind soil particles together and hence improve the **soil structure**.

Hybrid berries see **Cane fruit**.

Hygiene the practice of removing **pest**- or **disease**-infested plants or plant debris to prevent reinfection of future crops. For example, the spores of both rose **blackspot** and **apple scab** overwinter in fallen leaves, so getting rid of these before spring will help to prevent reinfection. Similarly, old brussels sprouts and **broccoli** plants left in the ground can host **whitefly** and **aphids**, which may then move on to your newly planted crops in spring.

Hygiene is essential in **greenhouses**: remove dead leaves from growing plants regularly and, in winter, wash the inside of the greenhouse and all your pots with hot, soapy water to help remove sources of infection. **Pruning** is also an important part of garden hygiene. Although a hot **compost heap** will destroy many diseases and pests, some, for example, the resistant spores of **clubroot**, will survive. If in doubt, burn infected debris or put it in the dustbin.

Ichneumon flies brown, leggy, flying insects, most of which
are **parasites** of **butterfly** and moth **caterpillars**. Ichneumons
are particularly helpful in controlling **cabbage caterpillars** in
the garden. The female lays her eggs inside the caterpillar.
These hatch into grubs, which parasitize the caterpillar,
killing it by the time they are fully grown. Encourage
ichneumons in the garden by growing **attractant plants**.
They particularly like flat, open **flowers**, for example,
single **asters**, **goldenrod**, and **umbellifers**, such as fennel.

Indicator species any native or naturalized plant whose
spontaneous presence can serve as an indication of physical conditions at a site, including **soil type**, the extent of
waterlogging, and any **mineral deficiencies**. For example,
salad burnet, *Sanguisorba minor*, indicates an **alkaline soil**,
and bracken, *Pteridium aquilinum*, an **acid soil**.

Inerts additives designed to enhance **pesticides'** effectiveness by increasing their ability to stick to plants or by
acting as carriers for the chemicals they contain. Of the
hundreds of inerts used in pesticides, little is known about
the majority of them, although some are known, or suspected, of being toxic. Despite this, they are rarely listed
on the pesticide label.

Insecticidal soap a specially formulated mixture of soap and
water, which is effective as an insecticidal spray, especially

against **aphids**, since it can destroy the waxy coating of their exoskeletons and kill them. It is one of the safest types of garden **spray** and acceptable in **organic gardening** because it is non-**persistent**, and kills only those creatures that it hits directly. This does not, however, rule out **beneficial insects** which may be in the area and be wiped out by a mistake. Other **pests** you can contain with insecticidal soap are **red spider mites, leafhoppers, thrips,** and **whitefly**.

Officially, the use of ordinary soapy water as an insecticide is illegal at present, because it has not undergone the full tests required for pesticide safety. Although you are unlikely to be prosecuted in practice for using soapy water in this way, commercially available, insecticidal-soap preparations are less likely to damage plants and are, in any case, often more effective.

Insecticide any **pesticide** that is used to kill insect **pests**. Some insecticides kill on contact, while others work by **systemic** means. Insecticides are probably the most commonly used type of pesticide worldwide. Unfortunately, they also tend to be the most hazardous, posing health risks to humans, pets, and wildlife, including many **beneficial insects**. No insecticide is completely "safe". **Derris** and **insecticidal soap** are two **natural insecticides** passed for use by organic gardeners.

Insecticide, natural see **Natural insecticide**.

Insects, beneficial see **Beneficial insects**.

Insects, harmful see **Pests**.

Insulation the practice of preventing loss or gain of heat. In a **greenhouse** or **conservatory**, good insulation, particularly in the form of draught exclusion, is vital in maintaining the correct temperature and conserving **energy**. In passive **solar heating** systems, thick masonry walls and floors and water-filled drums absorb heat and are important insulating devices. Some **compost bins** are made of insulating material, such as polystyrene sheets, designed to keep **compost** as warm as possible.

Integrated pest management (IPM) a **pest**-control strategy devised in the USA and increasingly in use throughout the rest of the world. IPM does not do away with the use of **pesticides** altogether, but instead employs them alongside **organic-gardening** methods, such as **cultural control**, **biological control**, **traps**, and **barriers**. IPM treats each pest problem as a distinct case, which needs careful analysis and a specially designed solution. Although not fully organic, many IPM programmes avoid the use of pesticides altogether, and there is much that organic gardeners can learn from this method.

Intensive gardening see **Bed system**.

Intensive
gardening

Intercropping

Interplanting

Iodofenphos

Ioxynil

Intercropping the sowing or planting of a quick-growing crop in the spaces between a slower maturing crop in order to make full use of the ground. Intercropping is also sometimes suggested as a form of **companion planting**, in which case the aim is to help prevent **pest** or **disease** attack rather than to save space.

   Always clear the quicker growing crop before the main crop begins to spread outward during its final stages of growth. **Radishes**, **lettuce**, and **spinach** are good fast crops to use. You can also try intercropping tall crops, such as **sweetcorn**, with low, trailing ones, for example, **marrows**, although it is not always easy to give both crops enough space, light, and moisture.

Interplanting see **Intercropping**.

Iodofenphos a **contact** and ingested **insecticide** of the **organophosphorus** group, used against **cabbage caterpillars**, **cabbage root fly**, and **onion fly**. It is a poison and an eye and skin **irritant**, with a **harvest interval** of seven to fourteen days. It is dangerous to **bees** and fish.

Ioxynil a **contact herbicide**, employed alone or in mixtures for general **weed control**. It is now no longer available for garden use, following tests which showed that it promoted birth defects in animals. It is a poison, a potential eye and skin **irritant**, and a suspected **mutagen** and **teratogen**. It is also dangerous to fish and can cause damage through **spray drift**. In the UK, you may still see old stock of ioxynil on sale in garden shops, and also agricultural ioxynil, which is still allowed in Britain although now banned in the USA. Try hand **weeding**, **hoeing**, or apply a **mulch** instead.

IPM see **Integrated pest management**.

Irrigation any method used to divert fresh water supplies to plants. If your garden is too large to carry out **watering** by hand, you will need to have an irrigation system. This is particularly neccessary if you are growing **fruit** and **vegetable** crops, since an adequate supply of water can make a tremendous difference both to yields and to the health of your plants. The main types of irrigation equipment to look out for are various types of **sprinkler** and **trickle system**; the latter helps to conserve water.

Irritant any substance that is capable of irritating the skin, eyes, and/or respiratory system; many irritants are also **allergens**. Irritation is one of the commonest health problems associated with **pesticides** and, in most cases, results in little more than mild hay-fever-like symptoms, for example, stinging, runny eyes. However, in sensitive people, irritants can cause much more serious allergic reactions and, sometimes, bad skin complaints, such as chloracne. If you are likely to come into contact with an irritant, you should wear full **protective clothing**, including gloves and a face mask. If a chemical splashes on to your skin, wash it off with plenty of cold water. If any gets into your eye, rinse it out thoroughly with cold water and consult a doctor immediately.

Ivy a plant, *Hedera helix*, native to Britain and much frequented by wildlife. It makes good **ground cover**, even in shady places, and its evergreen climbing stems give dense shelter for **birds** and many insects throughout the year. The flowers of mature ivy last into the winter, providing valuable late nectar for insects, while the berries do not ripen until late winter – a bonus for the birds at a time when most wild fruits have been eaten. Ivy will grow on most soils provided they are not waterlogged. It does not directly damage **walls** or **trees** on which it climbs, although it will compete with trees for water, air, and **nutrients**.

Kale see **Brassicas**.

Kitchen waste leftover food which you can add to the **compost heap** or use to feed chickens or pigs. Any **fruit** or **vegetable** scraps are suitable, but avoid adding diseased

material to the compost heap. Store the leftovers in a plastic bucket, emptying it on to the heap when full and washing it out thoroughly. Meat, cheese, and cooked food are likely to attract **rats** and **mice** so these are best given to the **birds**, unless you have a rat-proof **compost bin** or are using a **tumbler**. If you do keep chickens, you can feed most of your kitchen waste to them – their **nutrient**-rich **manure** will more than compensate for any lost **compost**. Alternatively, add the leftovers to a **wormbin**, an ideal way of composting small amounts of kitchen waste.

Knapsack sprayer a device, consisting of a tank and manual pump-action sprayer, which is used for applying large amounts of **pesticide** on a garden scale. Many knapsack sprayers are hazardous in terms of human contamination due to the risks of leakage, spillage, and **spray drift**.

Lacewings a group of **beneficial insects** (see p. 16), recognizable from their flimsy wings and delicate green or fawn bodies. Lacewing larvae are small, brown, and shuttle-shaped. Both adults and larvae eat **aphids**, but the adults also need a supply of nectar and pollen, which you can provide by growing **attractant plants**. The open, daisy-like flowers of the Compositae family are among the best, including single **asters**, pot **marigolds**, and **yarrow**.

Ladybirds a group of **beneficial insects** (see p. 16), the adult forms of which are usually red with black spots (most often two or seven in number), although you will see some with red spots on black and others with black spots on yellow. Ladybirds are voracious **aphid** eaters. The larvae are not so pretty but equally useful. They are longer and thinner, slatey blue with a few dull orange spots, and have an equal, if not greater, appetite for aphids.

You can encourage ladybirds by making sure your garden has some dry nooks and crannies for them to hibernate in. You will often find them in groups under loose bark or in old, hollow stems. You can also provide them with prey when they come out of hibernation by growing a patch of **nettles**: the aphids of the nettle do not attack other plants and are among the first to arrive in spring when other food is scarce.

Landscaping see **Design, garden**.

Lawn an area of short, regularly mown grass. Lawns do not have to be perfect grass swards. You should aim above all to keep the grass growing strongly: it will then stand up to wear, and **weeds** will not invade. Prepare for a new lawn by **clearing ground** of perennial weeds, by making sure **drainage** is adequate, and by digging in **organic matter**. Take care to choose a grass-seed mixture or turf that is suitable for your site. You can produce a fairly acceptable lawn on uncleared ground by frequent mowing, because only grasses and a few creeping or rosette-leaved **lawn weeds** will survive this treatment. See also **Wildflower meadow**.

Lawn maintenance various practices designed to maintain or improve the quality of an established **lawn**. Vigorous raking, or scarifying, with a machine designed for the purpose, will pull out any dead grass, or thatch, which can build up as a harmful layer on the **soil** surface. Spiking with a fork or machine will help to overcome **compaction**. You can also add a top dressing made up of a mixture of loam, sand, **leafmould**, and possibly **compost**, to improve the underlying **soil structure**. These are all annual operations which you should carry out in autumn. Regularly leaving your **lawn mowings** on the surface feeds the lawn, but an additional dressing of **natural fertilizer**, such as **seaweed meal**, may be necessary in spring.

 Moss growing on a lawn can indicate adverse conditions, such as waterlogging, an overly **acid soil**, poor fertility, and excess shade. It may also occur if the grass is mown too short. Correct any such imbalances and the moss should disappear. Rake out dead patches and sow with grass seed.

Lawn mowing the practice of regularly cutting **lawn** grass to maintain a smooth surface and to control **weed** growth. The way that you mow the grass can affect both the health and appearance of the lawn. First, do not cut it too short – 2.5cm (1in) is about right for a general purpose lawn. Secondly, cut it as soon as it needs it – at a height of around 3.75cm (1½in) – but not before, which may mean more than once a week in a wet summer, but not at all during periods of drought or cold. Finally, leave the mowings on the lawn to be taken under by **earthworms** and to maintain **soil fertility**. Collect them only in early spring when they will remain longer on the surface, or if you have let the grass grow too long.

Lawn
Lawn
maintenance
Lawn mowing

Lawn mowings recently cut young grass, which is high in **nitrogen** and a good **compost activator**. However, too many mowings in a **compost heap** will result in a sticky mass. Avoid this by adding fibrous material, such as chopped **straw** or autumn leaves. Alternatively, use the mowings as a **mulch** around **vegetable** crops, or leave them on the **lawn** to return **nutrients** to the **soil**.

Lawn weed any plant that successfully manages to avoid the mower blades. These will include low creeping plants, such as **yarrow**, and those that form a flat rosette of leaves, for instance, plantains. The best way to control them is through correct **lawn mowing** and **lawn maintenance**, which will ensure that the grass is healthy and provides plenty of competition. You will have to accept the presence of some weeds, but, even so, your **lawn** should look quite acceptable. It may even look greener in adverse conditions than an all-grass sward, and will support a greater variety of wildlife. The only way to remove lawn weeds without resorting to **herbicides** is by hand, either using a knife or one of the **tools** sold for the purpose.

Leaching the downward movement of chemicals through the **soil**, which can penetrate underground water sources. Some leaching occurs naturally, but intensive application of **fertilizers** and **manure** can lead to potentially hazardous levels of **nitrate** in soil and water. Leaching of **pesticides** can also reach pollutant levels.

Lead a heavy metal, which is extremely poisonous and can have a cumulative effect on the body, leading to brain damage and death; children are particularly vulnerable to lead poisoning. Lead may be present in the garden in old paint on wood work (which, if burnt, can leave high residues of lead in the ash), water pipes, as long-term residues from old **pesticides**, such as lead arsenate, and, most commonly, in vehicle exhaust emissions.

Airborne lead pollution from car exhausts remains a major concern for the urban gardener despite the availability of lead-free fuel, which has helped to reduce, but not so far to eliminate, the problem. Lead residues can, in any case, persist in the **soil** for thousands of years. Most **vegetables** do not take up large quantities through their roots, so the main contamination risks are from air-

Lawn mowings
Lawn weed
Leaching
Lead

borne lead settling on foliage, and soil deposits of lead building up on the outer skin of **root crops**. Most at risk are vegetables with large leafy areas, such as **lettuce**, **spinach**, and **cabbage**. Building up a good **humus** content through the use of **leafmould**, **compost**, and well-rotted **manure** can help bind lead in the soil and make it less available to plants. Correcting the **pH** balance is also important since lead is more mobile in **acid soils**.

After harvesting, you can get rid of some of the residues by taking off the outer leaves and thoroughly washing the rest. With root crops, for example, carrots, scraping or peeling will help to remove residues, but you will lose many valuable **nutrients** contained in the skin. Soft fruits with rough surfaces, such as **blackberries**, are particularly susceptible to lead contamination, so avoid picking any growing beside roads.

It is worth getting your soil tested for lead content if you are anywhere near a main road and, particularly, if you are going to be feeding garden vegetables to young children. Experts estimate that gardens most at risk are those that are 9m (30ft) or less away from busy roads. They also advise against growing outdoor food crops in inner cities, or at least not those with large leaves, which are most at risk. In highly polluted areas, grow plants under cover in a **greenhouse** or **cold frame**.

Leafhoppers
Leaf miners

Leafhoppers sap-feeding insects, similar to **froghoppers**, which attack a number of plants including **apples**, **strawberries**, **potatoes**, **raspberries**, and roses. They rarely cause significant damage, although some leafhopper species can carry **virus diseases**.

Leaf miners various types of grub, which tunnel within leaves, producing conspicuous markings, or "mines". The celery leaf miner, the larva of the celery fly, produces blotchy, brown blisters on the leaves of **celery** and some related plants. The beet leaf miner causes similar symptoms on **beetroot** and spinach beet plants, while the chrysanthemum leaf miner produces distinctive silvery, snake-like mines on the leaves of chrysanthemums. Bad attacks of leaf miner look unsightly and can weaken plants. Watch for the first signs of attack, and pick off infested leaves or squash the larvae within them. Growing plants under a protective **fleece** will prevent attacks.

Leafmould rotted autumn leaves used in **organic gardening** to improve the **soil structure**. To make leafmould, stack moist leaves somewhere where they will not blow away or dry out – in a wire mesh container, for example, or in plastic dustbin bags. Wait a year and the leafmould will be sufficiently rotted for you to use as a **mulch** or dig into the **soil**. It contains few **nutrients**, but it is slow to decay and invaluable for improving the soil structure. After two or three years, you will get a finer product, useful for dressing **lawns** or seedbeds, or for replacing the **peat** in **potting composts**. If you have room for three leafmould bins, this can give you good-quality material every year.

Leaf spots forms of spot **disease** that affect the leaves of plants and are caused by many different **fungi**, **viruses**, and **bacteria**. Often leaf spots do not seriously damage the plant, although they can make ornamentals unsightly. To prevent reinfection, practise good **hygiene**. Currant leaf spot, bean **chocolate spot**, and rose **blackspot** are among the commonest forms of leaf spot disease.

Leatherjackets the greyish brown, soil-living larvae of the familiar "daddy-long-legs", or crane fly. The larvae are common garden **pests**. The adults prefer grassy or weedy places to lay their eggs, so leatherjackets are mainly a problem in **lawns** and in plots recently brought into cultivation from pasture or weedy ground. Leatherjackets eat the roots of many different plants, including **brassicas**, **lettuces**, and **strawberries**, often causing them to wilt and die. They also cause yellow patches to occur on **lawns**. Regular cultivation of a new plot should gradually reduce the numbers of this pest. On lawns, you can sometimes encourage leatherjackets to come to the surface by **watering** the affected area thoroughly and placing black **polythene** on it overnight. You can then pick them off by hand.

Leeks see **Onions**.

Legumes plants of the Leguminosae family, whose fruits take the form of pods, for example, **peas** and **beans**. This group of plants has the ability to take in **nitrogen** from the air, and thus add to **nutrient** levels, through association with certain **bacteria** in the soil. Hence the importance of leguminous **green manures**, such as clover.

However, a particular legume will only fix nitrogen if the appropriate bacteria are present in the soil. In the UK, for example, runner and broad beans usually fix nitrogen but French beans do not. Commercial growers overcome this problem with some crops by adding innoculants containing **bacteria** to the soil or seed; a few innoculants are also available to gardeners.

Lettuce a valuable salad crop, available from the garden or **greenhouse** almost all year round in many regions. As well as the familiar cos and cabbage types, which produce tight heads, there are loose leaf lettuces, which will regrow several times after you cut them. Some are frilly or tinged with red and attractive enough for the edge of a **flower** border. Lettuce grows best in **soils** with plenty of **organic matter** and moisture. In summer they prefer light shade. If it is too hot, over 77°F (25°C), the seed of many **varieties** will not germinate. **Slugs**, **aphids**, and **root aphids** are the main lettuce **pests**, although there are varieties which have good **resistance** to root aphids. Downy **mildew** and **botrytis** are the most troublesome **diseases**, especially on winter crops grown under cover.

Lettuce
Lichen
Lime

Chicory and endives are related to lettuce and you should keep them together in any crop **rotation**. There are many types to give variety to winter salads, and most are much easier to grow in cold conditions than lettuce.

Lichen a plant formed from a complex symbiotic relationship between a fungus and an alga: each lichen species functions as a distinct organism but is actually made up of two very different types of plant. In many parts of Britain, the numbers of lichens have declined catastrophically due to **air pollution**, particularly by sulphur dioxide. In Epping Forest, near London, where there were 180 species of lichens a century ago, there are now only 36, and more than half of those will not grow in the area of forest that is nearest to London. Most species of lichen are very slow growing and pose no problem to the gardener, so try to avoid damaging them if at all possible.

Lime any of various naturally occurring **calcium** compounds, used for raising **soil pH** and thus making it less acid. You can buy lime in several different forms. Ground limestone and **dolomite** (which contains some **magnesium** as well as lime) are the best forms to use in **organic gardening**, because they are much slower acting than hydrated, or slaked, lime and last much longer in the soil.

Lindane another name for **gamma HCH**.

Liquid feed a type of **fertilizer**, which is watered on to the soil around a plant or sprayed on to its foliage. Organic liquid feeds include **comfrey** liquid, **nettle** liquid, and **liquid manure**. Although they are of natural origin, these feeds still tend to provide plants directly with **nutrients** in the same way that chemical liquid feeds do, rather than relying on soil **microorganisms** to break them down. They are no substitute for building up **soil fertility** and you should only use them regularly for plants grown in containers. You risk losing nutrients through **leaching** from use of liquid feeds on **vegetables** or **flower**beds.

Liquid manure a type of **liquid feed**, which contains a useful amount of **nutrients**. You can make it simply by suspending a sack of rotted **farmyard manure** in a barrel of water. There are no scientifically tested recipes: one of the best guides is that the resultant liquid should be the colour of weak tea. If it is much darker, you should dilute it to obtain the recommended colour before use.

Liquid seaweed see **Seaweed**.

Lizard a small, harmless reptile that lives under stones and in **walls** and is a good **natural predator**. Although shy, lizards do emerge to sun themselves in hot weather. If caught by a predator, they will shed their tails without suffering any permanent damage. You can attract lizards by leaving loose piles of rocks for them to shelter under.

Lupin, bitter a useful annual **green manure**, *Lupinus angustifolius*, which is smaller than the ornamental lupins. It is best sown in spring and summer, and dug in after two to three months before the flowers open (see **Green manures** chart, pp. 80-1). It is a **legume** and fixes **nitrogen** in the **soil**.

Machinery, garden any motor-powered device designed to facilitate, or replace the need for, manual labour. Much garden machinery is energy- and resource-expensive to manufacture and run, costly to buy, and noisy and potentially dangerous to operate. Think carefully before buying the latest gadget, and consider hiring rather than purchasing machinery for occasional heavy work. Keep any equipment you do have sharp and rust free, oiling blades and metal parts, when necessary. See also **Tools, garden**.

Magnesium an element, occurring in a number of compounds in the **soil**, and an important **nutrient** for plant growth. A healthy soil should contain sufficient quantities of magnesium, but you can use **seaweed fertilizers** or **dolomite** to top it up, if necessary. Magnesium deficiency · shows up as yellowing between the veins of leaves.

Malathion an **insecticide** and **acaricide** of the **organophosphorus** group, widely used to control **aphids** and **red spider mites**. It is poisonous if inhaled or absorbed through the skin and releases toxic gases at high temperatures. Malathion is an **anticholinesterase** compound, an eye and skin **irritant**, and an **allergen**. It is dangerous to **bees** and fish. It has a brief to moderate **persistence**, a **harvest interval** on edible crops of at least a day, and can damage some plants, including **peas**, ferns, antirrhinums, and orchids. Some aphids and red spider mites show **resistance** to malathion.

Maleic hydrazide a growth regulator and **herbicide** used against grass and some **weeds** on verges and near water, and against sucker growth on certain **trees**. It is an **irritant** and may release poisonous gases when heated. Evidence suggests that some formulations of it may be **carcinogens** and **mutagens**. Occasional scything (ideally after flowers have seeded) will keep verges under control, or you can mow regularly for a neater effect. Use clippers or a saw to remove tree suckers.

Mancozeb a **fungicide**, used alone or in mixtures against fungal attack on **potatoes**, **blackcurrants**, roses, **apples**, and **pears**; it is a complex of **maneb** and zinc. Mancozeb is a weak **irritant** and there is evidence that it is a **carcinogen** and **teratogen**. It is one of the **pesticides** being investigated by the US Environmental Protection Agency because of the potential health risks associated with its **residues** in food: these have been found to contain **ethylene thiourea**. Mancozeb has a **harvest interval** of at least one week and a long **persistence**. Try **cultural control** instead. Only resort to the safer fungicide, **Bordeaux mixture**, if all else fails. To improve on storage capacity of fruit, weed out bad specimens and stack carefully.

Maneb a **fungicide** used alone or in mixtures to control **potato and tomato blight**. Although maneb generally has low mammalian toxicity, it can cause adverse reactions in susceptible people: a 62-year-old-man suffered acute renal failure after using it in the garden. It is a potential skin, eye, and respiratory system **irritant**, and has been identified as a possible **carcinogen**. The US Environmental Protection Agency holds maneb **residues** under suspicion of being carcinogenic: storage or cooking of food containing them may produce **ethylene thiourea**. The EPA also lists maneb as a hazard to wildlife, and it is dangerous to fish. It has a **harvest interval** of at least a week and a long **persistence**. Use of maneb is banned in the USSR.

Manure a valuable form of **organic matter** for improving **soil structure** and **soil fertility**. Ideally, you should try to obtain manure from an organic farm, but in practice few have any to spare. Avoid manure produced by inhumane factory farms, for example, chicken manure from battery systems, which may be contaminated with antibiotics and heavy metals. Acceptable alternatives include **stable manure** from a riding school, **farmyard manure** from deep-litter cattle, and free-range **poultry manure**. Pigeon, rabbit, and goat manure is also suitable.

Most manures work best if mixed with **straw**, although poultry manure is rich in **nitrogen** and, alone, makes a good **compost activator**. When fresh, manure acts too quickly, is prone to **leaching**, and can burn plant leaves. It is therefore best to **compost** it before use by stacking it in a heap. Covering it with **polythene** will help to prevent leaching, and if you can leave it to rot for six months, this should allow any chemicals present time to break down into harmless by-products. Avoid applying manure in autumn, when there are fewer plants growing and leaching is more likely to occur; spring is the correct time.

Marigold, French a half-hardy annual, *Tagetes patula*, with multicoloured flowers in shades of orange, red, and yellow. French marigolds are usually grown as bedding plants, but they are also sometimes used as a **companion plant** in **greenhouses** because they have the reputation of keeping away **whitefly**.

Marigold, pot a hardy annual, *Calendula officinalis*; also called calendula. Single **varieties** have daisy-like, orange, or yellow flowers and are good **attractant plants**, particularly for **hoverflies**. They are also loved by **bees**. They like sun, and will readily self-seed.

Marrows see **Squashes**.

Maximum Residue Limit the maximum amount of **pesticide residue** that is permitted to remain on **fruit** and **vegetables** when they are sold to eat. The limit is set according to European Community regulations.

MCPA a **translocated herbicide** used against broad-leaved **weeds** and plants other than food crops. MCPA is a poison and can be toxic if swallowed, inhaled, or absorbed through the skin – it has caused several human fatalities. It is an **irritant** and according to the UN International Labour Organisation can cause severe contact **dermatitis**. There is evidence that it may be a **mutagen**. MCPA can cause damage through **spray drift** and through applications

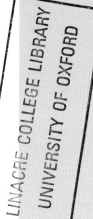

of **compost** made from treated grass clippings. Use hand **weeding**, **hoeing**, forking, or apply a **mulch** instead.

MCPP see **Mecoprop**.

Mealybug a small, sap-feeding insect (see p. 17) and a **greenhouse pest**. It often attacks vines and ornamental plants. Colonies cluster together, and protect themselves with a white, waxy powder. Reduce damage by cutting out infested shoots and branches, washing plants with a jet of water, or removing the pests with a paint brush.

Mecoprop a **translocated herbicide**, used alone or in mixtures against a wide range of broad-leaved **weeds**. It is poison-ous if swallowed, inhaled, or absorbed through the skin, an eye, skin, and respiratory system **irritant**, and there is some evidence that it may be a **mutagen**. There is a risk of damage from **spray drift**. Use hand **weeding**, **hoeing**, forking, or apply a **mulch** instead.

Melon a half-hardy, trailing plant, cultivated for its succu-lent fruit. Melons are best grown in the **greenhouse** or under **cloches** in a cool climate. Melons are related to **cucumbers** and need similar growing methods.

Mercurous chloride a **fungicide** used mainly against **clubroot** but also on turf; otherwise known as calomel. Mercurous chloride is a poison, an eye and skin **irritant**, and may release toxic gases when heated. It is one of the most dan-gerous **pesticides**. The International Labour Organisation states that it can cause permanent damage to the nervous system. "Calomel sickness", characterized by fever and a rash, can sometimes occur about a week after exposure. Mercurous chloride is very toxic to all forms of wildlife and to pets, and has a long **persistence**. It has been severely restricted in the European Community, and in 1986 was withdrawn from use on turf.

Metabolite any substance participating in, or produced as a result of, metabolic processes within an organism. **Pesti-cides** may be the source of metabolites once inside the cells of plants or animals. **Carbendazim**, for example, is a metabolite of the pesticide, **benomyl**. Some relatively harmless pesticides can result in toxic metabolites.

Metaldehyde a **molluscicide** used to control **slugs** and **snails**. It is a poison and can cause vomiting, fever, diarrhoea, convulsions, and coma. In one instance, a child died after eating only 3g of this poison. Metaldehyde is extremely dangerous to a wide range of animals and is responsible for many deaths among pets, **hedgehogs**, **frogs**, **toads**, and **birds**. It is harmful to fish and has a **harvest interval** of ten days. See **Slugs** for safer, alternative methods of control.

Methane a gas released naturally from rotting vegetation in marshy areas, but also the product of certain farming practices. In rice-paddy cultivation, for example, the rotting plants release methane, while in farming, concentrations of ruminating animals can give off the gas.

The quantity of methane in the atmosphere is increasing and it is now considered to be a major air pollutant, contributing to **global warming**. It does, however, have its uses, being a principal constituent of natural gas and potential source of **energy**. In theory, you can produce it together with a liquid slurry, which is used as a **natural fertilizer**, by allowing plant and animal waste to undergo **anaerobic bacterial decomposition** in a methane digester. In practice however, this is not feasible since no models have yet been suitably developed for garden use.

Methiocarb a **molluscicide** of the **carbamate** group, used against **slugs** and **snails**. It is a poison with high oral toxicity, and an **anticholinesterase** compound. Methiocarb is dangerous to all wildlife, fish, and to pets, and has a **harvest interval** of at least a week. See **Slugs** for safer, alternative methods of control.

Methoxone another name for **Mecoprop**.

Methyl bromide a highly toxic **soil** fumigant, available only in mixtures in Britain, usually with chloropicrin. Prolonged exposure to this chemical can present serious health risks. It is a poison, which is very toxic if inhaled, and an **irritant**, which can cause severe damage to the eyes. It is highly toxic to all forms of wildlife, pets, and **bees**, and to fish. Methyl bromide is one of the pollutants currently responsible for damaging the **ozone** layer. It is also very damaging to the **soil**, and thus goes against the basic principles of **organic gardening**. Try **cultural control** instead.

Metaldehyde
Methane
Methiocarb
Methoxone
Methyl bromide

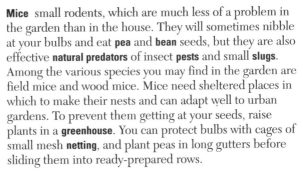

Mice small rodents, which are much less of a problem in the garden than in the house. They will sometimes nibble at your bulbs and eat **pea** and **bean** seeds, but they are also effective **natural predators** of insect **pests** and small **slugs**. Among the various species you may find in the garden are field mice and wood mice. Mice need sheltered places in which to make their nests and can adapt well to urban gardens. To prevent them getting at your seeds, raise plants in a **greenhouse**. You can protect bulbs with cages of small mesh **netting**, and plant peas in long gutters before sliding them into ready-prepared rows.

Microclimate a local variation in climatic factors as found, for example, under a **tree**, between closely planted **vegetables**, or beside a **pond**. You need to get to know the various microclimates in your garden in order to work out which plants will thrive in them. Take note, for example, of any places that tend not to be affected by **frost**, and use these areas for plants that cannot survive low temperatures.

Microorganism any living plant or animal that is invisible to the naked eye. Microorganisms include **bacteria**, unicellular algae, some **fungi**, and single cell animals, such as amoebae; many of these have important roles to play in the garden **ecology**. To ensure a healthy **soil** and to make the best use of beneficial microorganisms as well as minimizing the effects of harmful ones, practise **cultural control**.

Mildew see **Mildew, downy** and **Mildew, powdery**.

Mildew, downy a **disease** caused by several different related **fungi**, each attacking only one group of plants. Typical symptoms include yellow patches on the surface of leaves and off-white or purplish moulds on the undersides. Crops affected include **brassicas**, **onions**, **beetroot**, **peas**, **celery**, **parsnips**, **spinach**, and **lettuce**. The disease is commonest in cool, damp weather. The spores of the fungi can survive in the **soil**, on crop debris, and on growing plants. Good **hygiene** is an essential preventative measure, and you should also use a long **rotation**. Do not crowd plants, and thin seedlings early. Maintain good ventilation in **greenhouses** and avoid getting water on plant leaves. Remove and destroy infected plants. Look out for **resistant varieties** of, for example, peas and lettuce.

Mildew, powdery a widespread **disease** attacking many **fruit** and **vegetable** crops, and ornamentals. It is caused by various **fungi**, each attacking a different group of plants, but all producing the characteristic thin, white coating on leaves and stems. They are most active when the weather is warm and dry, and on dry **soils**. Commonly affected are **apples**, **gooseberries**, **blackcurrants**, **strawberries**, **brassicas**, **cucumbers** and related plants, **peas**, roses, and a variety of other ornamental plants. Most powdery mildews survive on crop debris.

To avoid problems, ensure that plants do not go short of water. Grow **resistant varieties** where available (for example, of **swedes**, peas, gooseberries, and apples). With apples, prune out previously mildewed shoots which are distorted and discoloured. Remove affected gooseberry tips, and keep the bushes open and well spaced.

Mildew, powdery

Millipede

Mineral

Mineral deficiency

Millipede a slim, multi-legged, segmented invertebrate, which is a common garden **pest** (see p. 17). Millipedes have two pairs of legs per segment and are not to be confused with **centipedes**, which have only one; they also move more slowly. Millipedes feed principally on dead plant material but they also eat seeds and young seedlings, and will enlarge wounds made by other creatures in tubers, bulbs, and roots. Search for the pests in the **soil** surrounding damaged plants. You may be able to distract them from seedlings by using **traps** made from pieces of **potato** or **carrot**, stuffed into a perforated tin can. Bury these in the soil and empty and replace them regularly.

Mineral any solid inorganic substance, including many valuable plant **nutrients** and **trace elements**.

Mineral deficiency an insufficient supply of a particular **nutrient** to a plant. This usually results in visual symptoms which are sometimes easily recognizable. For example, yellowing between the veins of **tomato** leaves is usually a sign of **magnesium** deficiency. However, sometimes, deficiency may simply be indicated by poor growth or a lack of flowers or fruit. Signs of a deficiency of a particular **mineral** do not necessarily mean that it is not present in the **soil**. Sometimes an "overdose" of one mineral can prevent the plant taking up others, and sometimes the **pH** of the soil is to blame. **Soil testing** will usually highlight any such problems. In general, however, plants grown on an organically managed soil are less likely to suffer from mineral deficiencies because the nutrients present in **manure** and **natural fertilizers** are well balanced, and are released gradually in step with the needs of the plants.

Mites see **Red spider mite**.

Mole a small, virtually blind mammal, which feeds on insect larvae, **beetles**, **slugs**, and **earthworms**. Moles can spoil your **lawn** with their burrows and hills, and can also damage **flower** and **vegetable** beds. Should they cause unacceptable damage, then the only really viable option is to employ a professional mole catcher, who will use **traps** to catch them. However, there are various sound-based folk remedies you can try, which are intended to scare them away, including positioning of toy windmills or other commercially available sound devices, over the burrows.

Molluscicide a **pesticide** used to kill **slugs** and **snails**. Most molluscicides are poisonous to pets and garden wildlife, including **natural predators**, and hazardous to children. See **Slugs** for safer, alternative methods of control.

Monoculture a single crop grown over a large area, often for a number of years. Monocultures are very prone to **pests** and **diseases**, since they provide ideal conditions – large expanses of a single crop – in which a pest or pathogen can build up its numbers without competition. Particular **weeds** which fit in with the growing cycle of the crop also flourish, and the **fertility** of the **soil** is depleted because the same **nutrients** are always in demand. In a garden, try to get as far away from a monoculture as possible by introducing many different food crops, together with **shrubs**, **herbs**, and **flowers**, and by planning a **rotation**.

Mosquito a flying, bloodsucking insect, whose bite can give humans a nasty bump on the skin, but nothing more serious than that outside the malarial areas of the world. If you have a **pond** or other area of standing water in your garden, such as a **water butt**, you may be providing a breeding site for mosquitoes. They produce wormlike larvae, each with a cluster of tiny hairs at one end, which hang motionless over the surface of the water and react to disturbances by swimming around with thrashing movements. If you want to reduce mosquitoes in the garden, you can begin by scooping them off the surface of any standing water. You can also cover water butts to prevent mosquitoes using them as breeding grounds.

Moss a group of primitive plants, in the Bryophyte class. Many mosses are, like **lichens**, susceptible to **air pollution** and numbers have declined in industrial areas of Britain. Mosses will come into your garden of their own accord if conditions are right, for example, around a **pond** or in the damp part of a rockery. Do not transplant species from the wild because they will almost certainly die. (Digging up of wild plants is in any case illegal in Britain.) Moss can be a nuisance if it overtakes your **lawn**, and may indicate such adverse conditions as waterlogging, poor fetility, high acidity, or too closely mown grass. See **Lawn maintenance** for methods of controlling moss on lawns.

Moss killers specialized **herbicides** used to kill **moss** on **lawns**; these are often mixed with artificial **fertilizers** and sold as general lawn treatments. The use of moss killers is unacceptable in **organic gardening**. See **Lawn maintenance** for alternative methods of moss control on lawns.

Mowings see **Lawn mowings**.

MRL acronym for **Maximum Residue Limit**.

Mulch a layer of material used to cover the **soil**. Putting down a mulch is valuable for a number of reasons including: controlling **weeds**; keeping moisture in the soil; helping the **soil structure**; adding **nutrients**; and keeping plants clean and **disease** free.

The effect of a mulch will depend on the material you use. Non-degradable mulches such as black **plastic** film are the best for **clearing ground** of weeds, and you can also use them for warming the soil in spring or keeping it cool in summer. Gravel is a useful mulch for keeping plants, such as low, shrubby **herbs**, clean.

Possible mulches of **organic matter** include **compost**, **manure**, **hay**, **straw**, **leafmould**, **lawn mowings**, shredded **bark**, and **woodchips**. When nutrients are required, for example, around **brassicas** and **blackcurrant** bushes, choose those

Use nature's colours, sounds, scents, and textures in the ways suggested below to create your own garden of the senses.

Bee and butterfly plants Include plants, such as catmint, sedum, lavender, and scabious for the hum of the **bees** collecting nectar and the colour of the **butterflies** as they feed and sun themselves.

Bird bath and bird table Encourage **birds** for their song by providing them with food, water, and places to shelter.

Patio For visual and textural effect, set stone paving slabs in colourful **ground cover**.

Statue A small stone statuette acts as a focal point.

Pond and water-loving plants An area of still water has a soothing effect. Surround it with velvety bullrushes and spiky teasels for shape, texture, and colour.

Dry-stone wall and seat Cover a low stone wall with aromatic plants, such as thyme and artemesias, and position those with a furry texture close to the seat at hand level.

Blue and white flowers Group blue and white annuals and perennials, including scented nicotiana flowers that open in the evening and attract moths.

Pergola with scented climbers Create a perfumed, covered walkway by training scented, climbing roses over a line of archways.

Native tree A native silver birch gives dappled shade. For a striking alternative, try the twisted hazel *Corylus avellana contorta*. When leafless, it has a fascinating contorted shape, with catkins toward the end of the winter.

Woodland edge area Include native, woodland plants, such as foxglove and woodruff, and naturalized bulbs.

Old tree trunk Tree bark provides a contrast of rough and smooth areas to touch, as well as nooks and crannies for all sorts of creatures.

Shrubs Plant shrubs with coloured bark in winter, such as **dogwood**, and early flowering viburnum species.

Red and orange flowers Simple, bright annuals, such as pot **marigold** and rudbeckia, are visually striking and good **attractant plants** for **hoverflies** and other **beneficial insects**.

Foliage plants Combine greens of various shades and textures and apply a dark mulch for a contrast in colour and texture.

Grasses Tall grasses will stand out and whisper in the wind.

Lawn An area of mown grass is somewhere where you can relax and the birds can feed.

Trellis A simple trellis-work screen will hide the composting area. Cover it with attractive, evergreen berried shrubs, such as **pyracantha**.

such as compost and manure. Longer lasting mulches, for instance, weathered, shredded bark are more appropriate around **shrubs** or other areas where the soil is never disturbed. A thick layer, about 10cm (4in) in depth, will help stop weed seeds from germinating, but will not control existing perennial weeds. All these mulches help to protect the soil surface, keep in moisture, and eventually add **organic matter** to the soil as they are taken under by **earthworms**. However, they can also provide cover for a variety of **pests**, including **slugs** and **snails**.

Municipal compost large-scale production of **compost** from **household waste**. In Britain, a few local authorities, for example, Birmingham, are experimenting with municipal composting, but the practice is still relatively rare when compared with some European countries. Switzerland and Germany, for example, practice it on a large scale: household waste is sorted before collection and **biodegradable** material composted at large municipal units. The resultant compost is then sold to gardeners and farmers.

Mushroom compost a by-product of commercial mushroom growing, which can make a useful soil conditioner and also supply some plant **nutrients**. Unfortunately, it has some drawbacks. Although mainly made up of rotted **stable manure**, it is mixed with **peat**, and also contains a lot of **lime**. Thus, you should not overuse it and, if your **soil** is **alkaline**, you should avoid it altogether. It may also contain **residues** of **persistent pesticides**, which mushroom growers use. This makes it unsuitable for **organic gardening** unless you store it for six months to give them the chance to decompose.

Mustard an annual **green manure**, *Sinapis alba*, and one of the quickest growing. You can sow it anytime from March to September. Dig it in before it flowers in summer (possibly after only three to four weeks). You can also leave it in the ground during a mild winter and it should survive (see **Green manures** chart, pp.80-1). Dig it in before it flowers. It is related to **brassicas** and is susceptible to **clubroot**.

Mutagen any substance or process which causes changes, or mutations, in genetic material. Many mutagens are also **carcinogens** and **teratogens**. See **Carcinogen** for a discussion of the problems involved in their identification.

Nasturtium an annual, *Tropaeolum majus*, which is a good **attractant plant**. The flowers are red, orange, or yellow, appearing in summer and early autumn. It likes poor **soils** and sunny sites, and will only tolerate slight **frosts**.

Native plant any plant that is indigenous to a particular region. Native plants help to increase **diversity**, and will attract more wildlife than introduced plants. You can grow almost any wild plant if you have the right conditions. Some of the most attractive and easy-to-grow species include primroses, bluebells, cowslips, foxgloves, corn marigolds, and cornflowers. Do not dig up wild plants because this will destroy natural plant communities and is illegal in Britain. A number of specialist seed dealers supply seeds of wildflowers, reared in nurseries, and there are special hay-meadow mixtures available if you want a lawn that contains more than just grass, or a **wildflower meadow**. Buy native seeds where possible because the resultant plants will be better adapted to local conditions.

Natural fertilizers concentrated sources of **nutrients** which are of plant or animal origin, for example, **hoof and horn meal**, **seaweed**, and **bone meal**. These differ from chemical **fertilizers** in that they have to be broken down by **bacteria** in the soil before they are available, rather than feeding the plants directly. They also each contain a mixture of nutrients, including some of the minor and **trace elements**. ▷

115

Plant roots and **soil** bacteria both require warmth and moisture to be active and, when conditions are right, the bacteria will release nutrients from natural fertilizers at about the time that plant roots are ready to take them up. Natural fertilizers are thus more likely to be in step with the needs of plants than artificial fertilizers, and are less likely to be washed out of the soil by rain, but they are not a proper substitute for building up the **soil fertility** with **manures** and other forms of **organic matter**. However, together with **rock fertilizers**, they are useful for correcting inherent **mineral deficiencies** in the soil. They can also supply readily available nutrients while you build up the health of the soil, particularly in the case of long-term crops, such as **tree** and **bush fruit**.

Natural insecticide any naturally derived insecticide designed to do the least harm to users and the environment and, as a result, approved of by organic gardeners. Natural insecticides break down quickly into non-active substances, so that they hit the **pest** which you spray, but do not persist to harm **beneficial insects**, which may come along afterward. Examples include **derris** and **insecticidal soap**.

Although these insecticides are of natural origin, this does not mean that any natural substance is suitable. **Nicotine** is a good example of one that is not due to its potential toxicity. Another, **pyrethrum**, is frequently adulterated and you may have difficulty finding a pure form suitable for use in **organic gardening**. There are a variety of other home-made **sprays** which gardeners use: those made from **rhubarb** or **elder**, for example. However, these are in fact illegal. All pesticides have to be approved by the Ministry of Agriculture after rigorous safety tests and, of course, home-made sprays have never been submitted for approval. Only use natural insecticides as a last resort, when other preventative methods have failed and pest damage is likely to be severe.

Natural predators wild creatures of any size that prey on garden **pests**. They include **ladybirds**, which feast on **aphids**, starlings, which pick **leatherjackets** off the **lawn**, and **hedgehogs**, which help control **slugs**. Encouraging natural predators into your garden by providing them with sources of food and natural shelter is an important part of **biological control**.

Nature gardening an **organic gardening** technique in which the emphasis is on encouraging wildlife to visit and live in your garden (see The Nature Garden, pp. 144-5). You can simply add a **bird table** and **nest boxes** or turn your whole garden into a miniature nature reserve. Elements to consider incorporating include: boxes for **bats** and **hedgehogs** as well as **birds**; **native plant** species; a **wildflower meadow**; a **pond**; and some areas of rough vegetation as well as piles of logs and stones for insects and small mammals. In **organic gardening**, a good "reservoir" of wildlife is essential as a source of **natural predators** for **pest** control. Wildlife gardens can provide an important haven for common species which have declined in recent years.

Neck rot a common **disease** of stored **onions**, which can also affect **shallots** and **garlic**. A soft rot starts in the neck of the bulb and then spreads through it. The disease is mainly to be found in infected seed, but sets and crop debris can also carry it. To reduce the likelihood of neck rot, practise good **hygiene** and use a three- to four-year **rotation** of crops. Do not overfeed plants or use overhead **irrigation**, since this makes them prone to rot. Wait for their leaf tops to fall over naturally before harvesting, then dry the bulbs and store them in a cool, dry, airy place.

Nematodes see **Eelworms**.

Nest boxes wooden boxes that provide both roosting and nesting sites for **birds** in areas where there is insufficient natural cover. These boxes can make a very real difference to the numbers of certain species if put in the right places. In Wales, for example, they are thought to be one of the main reasons for the recovery in populations of pied fly-catchers. There are various designs appropriate for different bird species. Blue tits and great tits need an entrance hole of no more than 28mm ($1^1/_8$ in), otherwise they will be pushed out by the more aggressive house sparrow, whereas wrens like open boxes in sheltered places. Be sure to position nest boxes where they are inaccessible to cats. See **Bat** and **Hedgehog** for information on building boxes for these creatures.

Netting lightweight, openwork material, used to protect plants from scavengers and **pests**. Ordinary plastic garden netting, with an approximate 2cm (⁴⁄₅in) mesh, is useful for keeping **birds** off soft **fruit** and seedbeds. You should, however, always remove it in winter to allow birds to help with pest control. You can also use smaller mesh netting, with holes of 1cm (²⁄₅in) or less, to protect **brassica** plants against the large and small white **butterfly**. Burying the bottom of wire netting 30cm (12in) in the ground is one of the few ways to keep out **rabbits**.

Nettle
Newspaper
Newt

Nettle a plant, commonly considered a **weed**, but with multiple uses in **organic gardening**. You can use it for making **liquid feed**, as a **compost activator**, and for attracting **beneficial insects**. To make the liquid feed, soak about 1kg (2.2lb) of nettles in a barrel of water for a few weeks. Use the resultant "nettle water", which contains useful amounts of plant **nutrients**, directly from the barrel. Nettle aphids are among the earliest to appear in spring, when they provide food for **beneficial insects**, such as **ladybirds**, waking up from hibernation. Several **butterflies**, including peacocks, small tortoiseshells, and red admirals, lay their eggs almost exclusively on nettle leaves.

Newspaper a **biodegradable** material with a wide range of uses in **organic gardening**. You can add it directly to the **compost heap**, although it should not make up more than 10% of the total, and needs to be torn into pieces. Newspaper also makes a useful **weed**-suppressing **mulch** around widely spaced **vegetables**. If you are importing **soil** to make new beds, a thick layer of newspaper or **cardboard** underneath can help to prevent **nutrients leaching** while the soil is building up its **humus** content. Do not use glossy paper, which will take a long time to rot, or brightly coloured paper, which may contain toxic dyes.

Newt a harmless amphibian which needs water if it is to breed but which spends most of the year living in damp vegetation and hibernates over the winter. Newts eat a number of garden **pests**, including **slugs**. Newt numbers are declining at present and a good way of protecting them is to provide an additional habitat in the form of a **pond**. The great crested newt is particularly at risk and is also the one which eats the most pests, so this species is especially welcome. If you are interested in getting newts to breed in your garden, contact your local English

Nature office (see Useful Addresses, pp. 190-1) for advice. Do not take them from the wild.

New Zealand box a type of **compost bin**, which is ideal for a medium-sized garden. It is made out of wood, roughly 1m (3ft 3in) cubed, with solid sides and a sloping roof. For DIY instructions on how to make a New Zealand Box, contact the Henry Doubleday Research Association (see Useful Addresses, pp. 190-1).

Nicotine a **natural insecticide**, used against a wide range of **vegetable** and **fruit pests**. Despite its traditional use as a garden **spray**, nicotine is in fact highly toxic. It is classified as "highly hazardous" by the World Health Organisation, is poisonous if swallowed or inhaled, and is rapidly absorbed through the skin, so you should wash off any splashes immediately. Nicotine is a **carcinogen** and **teratogen**. It can also affect the nervous system, although risks are apparently greater for non-smokers who have not built up any immunity. Nicotine is dangerous to all animals and has a **harvest interval** of two days. In the USA, most formulations of nicotine have been restricted to use by certified operators only. If you have to use a **natural insecticide**, there are safer types, such as **derris** and **insecticidal soap**.

New Zealand box
Nicotine
Nitrate
Nitrogen

Nitrate a principal component of many artifical **fertilizers**, which is used to supply **nitrogen**. Extensive use of artificial fertilizers has led to an increase in the amount of nitrate **leaching**, resulting in rising levels in water and a build-up of **residues** in some **vegetables**, such as **lettuce** and **spinach**. Nitrate can pollute rivers and the sea, contributing to algal blooms and oxygen deprivation. Opinion is divided over the seriousness of nitrate leaching and residues. High levels in water can cause a potentially fatal condition in infants under three months, known as methaemoglobinaema, or blue baby syndrome, although there have only ever been a handful of cases in Britain, the last over twenty years ago. Equally serious are laboratory tests linking nitrate to stomach cancer, although studies of human populations have so far failed to confirm this link.

Nitrogen an essential **nutrient** for plant growth. In **organic gardening**, you can use **legumes** in a **rotation** to help raise nitrogen levels. These have the ability to fix nitrogen from

the air, so long as the correct **bacteria** are present in the **soil**. **Manure**, **urine**, and some **natural fertilizers** are rich in readily available nitrogen, as are certain **composts** and **liquid feeds**, in particular those made with **comfrey** and **nettles**.

Intensive use of artificial **fertilizers** frequently results in an excess of nitrogen in the form of **nitrate**, which can leach away into freshwater systems and build up to unnaturally high levels in food crops. In addition, some of the nitrogen from artificial fertilizers, and possibly also from some manures, can transform into nitrogen oxides, which are major air pollutants. The use of natural fertilizers and manure can also result in **leaching** of nitrogen if applied at the wrong time of year, for instance, in autumn when there are fewer growing plants to take up nutrients.

Maintaining a good **soil structure** with **cultural control** and only using natural fertilizers when necessary will help to reduce the amount of nutrients lost. To prevent leaching and maintain nutrient levels in autumn months, sow a **green manure** crop, such as **mustard**, on any bare ground.

Nutrients foods required by plants, which they obtain from two sources – the air and the **soil**. Plant leaves take in carbon dioxide from the air for photosynthesis, and the roots generally absorb all the other nutrients the plant needs from the soil. The main nutrients that plants require in relatively large quantities are **nitrogen**, **phosphorus**, and **potassium**. They also need moderate amounts of **calcium**, **sulphur**, and **magnesium**, and minute quantities of **trace elements**, such as iron and zinc. Some of these nutrients are found in the **mineral** particles of the **soil**, but mostly they come from **organic matter**. This is broken down by soil **microorganisms**, which release the nutrients in a simple form to be taken up by plants.

Oak a hardwood **tree** of the genus *Quercus*, with over 300 insect species associated with it. If you buy an oak from a nursery, check that you are buying one of the two species native to Britain, *Quercus robor* or *Q. petraea*. Alternatively, grow your own from acorns of these species. Oaks are slow growing so you will not live to see a full grown tree, but future generations will thank you. The trees grow tall, so only allow them to mature if you have a large garden. In a small garden, you can plant oak as part of a mixed **hedge**, or keep it small by **coppicing** it.

Oncogenic describing any substance that causes tumours, which may be benign or malignant.

Onion a common garden **vegetable**, cultivated for its edible bulb. Onions require similar growing conditions to other members of the genus *Allium*, for example, leeks, garlic, and shallots. Keep these related plants together in your crop **rotation**. They all need a sunny, well-drained site and a **soil** rich in **organic matter**. Given these conditions, they are generally easy to grow, and can provide you with an all-year-round supply from the garden.

   Main crop onions are harvested in autumn. Those grown from seed keep longer than those from sets, and you get a better choice of **varieties**. Supplement these types of onion with overwintering varieties which mature in early summer, and with successive sowings of spring onions.

   Leeks are a hardy crop, which you can harvest throughout the winter in most regions. Garlic is also hardy and will produce bulbs for harvesting in midsummer from an autumn planting of individual cloves.

   The main problems affecting onions and related plants are **onion fly**, **white rot**, and **rust**, although for rust there are **resistant varieties**. Stored bulbs are affected by **neck rot**.

Onion fly a small, grey fly, which is a **pest** of **onions**, shallots, and leeks, laying its eggs on or near a crop. The emerging white maggots feed on the crop's roots, killing young plants and causing older ones to rot. They then pupate in the **soil**. There may be two or three generations of this pest within a year. You can help prevent attacks by **digging** over infected land in winter to expose the pupae, and by crop **rotation**. Placing a protective **fleece** over the crop should prevent the fly from laying its eggs.

Onion white rot see **White rot**.

Organic based describing products that contain a mix of organic and chemical components. A common example is that of organic-based "complete" **fertilizers**, which provide a balance of **nitrogen**, **phosphorus**, and **potassium**. These frequently contain a chemical source of potassium because it is hard to supply in its natural form, although the other ingredients may be organic. You should avoid using such products in an organic garden.

Organic gardening a gardening philosophy and practice that aims to create a healthy, balanced environment in which plants can thrive. This implies more than just gardening without chemical **fertilizers** and **pesticides.** Fundamentally, it means working with nature rather than against it.

First, you should build up the **soil fertility** by **recycling organic matter** – a system that involves feeding the **soil** and all the living creatures it contains, rather than the plants directly. Secondly, you should introduce **diversity** into the garden to attract as much wildlife as possible, particularly **beneficial insects** and other **natural predators**. This will help to keep **pest** populations in balance with those of their enemies and prevent them from building up to damaging levels. For a specific pest or **disease** problem, there are various measures you can adopt, including **biological control**, **cultural control**, **barriers**, and **traps**. You can also use **natural fertilizers** and **natural insecticides** to assist you, particularly when you are establishing an organic garden, but not as a matter of course. Instead, you need to build up an understanding of the garden **ecology** and to find ways of preventing problems arising.

Organic gardening
Organic matter
Organic seeds

Organic matter any bulky material of living origin, such as **manure**, leaves and **leafmould**, **straw**, **hay**, plant debris, **household scraps**, and **seaweed**. In **organic gardening**, such materials are recycled back to the **soil** by adding them to a **compost heap** or **wormbin**, by digging them directly into the soil, or by using them as a **mulch**. Organic matter is vital to the **soil structure**, and will slowly be broken down by microscopic creatures to release a supply of plant **nutrients**. The value of a particular material will depend on how quickly it breaks down and how many nutrients it contains. Soft materials, such as seaweed, are rich in nutrients. Longlasting materials, for example, leafmould are more useful in improving soil structure. Some materials, such as straw, decay fairly quickly and have a high **carbon-nitrogen ratio**. This can cause depletion of **nitrogen** if you dig them into the soil, but they are still valuable as mulches.

Organic seeds seed that has been produced by organically grown plants. If you cannot buy organic seed, you can do some **seed saving** yourself. This is worthwhile with some crops and **flowers** but not practical with all of them. The next best thing is to use seed which, although not organic, is free from the chemical dressing usually applied after harvesting. A few seed companies guarantee this.

Organochlorine an organic compound containing chlorine; many of the most hazardous **pesticides** are organochlorines, for example, aldrin, DDT, and **gamma HCH**. Organochlorines are extremely **persistent** and can circulate in food chains. Many are toxic to humans and other animals.

Organophosphorus one of the older classes of **insecticide**. Although generally less **persistent** than the **organochlorines**, organophosphorus **pesticides** tend to be more hazardous to both health and the environment. They include **demeton-s-methyl**, diazinon, and **fenitrothion**.

Oxycarboxin a systemic **fungicide** used against **rusts**. It is a skin and eye **irritant**. Oxycarboxin is moderately **persistent** in the **soil** and dangerous to **fish**. At least one strain of **fungus** shows **resistance**. Try **cultural control** instead.

Oxydemeton methyl a **systemic insecticide** and **acaricide** of the **organophosphorus** group, used to control **aphids**, **red spider mites**, apple and plum **sawflies**, and the pear sucker. It is a poison and **anticholinesterase** compound and is highly dangerous to all animals, including **bees** and fish, remaining toxic for at least two weeks following application. It has a **harvest interval** of around three weeks. In Britain, oxydemeton methyl is no longer used in gardens, although old stock may still be available.

Ozone a form of oxygen with three atoms in each molecule instead of the usual two. Ozone is a vital component of the upper atmosphere, the stratosphere, forming a protective layer that filters ultraviolet radiation from the sun, excesses of which can cause skin cancer in humans. Stratospheric ozone is currently being destroyed by some types of air pollutant, notably **CFCs**.

Paradoxically, other air pollutants are creating too much ozone in the atmosphere near ground level, where high levels are damaging crops and **trees**. In particular, some of the components of vehicle exhausts react with sunlight during hot summer months, producing harmful levels of ozone in rural areas.

Organochlorine
Organophos-
phorus
Oxycarboxin
Oxydemeton
methyl
Ozone

Paradichlorobenzene an **insecticide** used against mites in
house and garden. It is highly toxic and has been reported
as causing cancers in laboratory animals and liver injury in
humans following chronic exposure. It is dangerous to
aquatic life, and is **persistent** in water. Try **cultural control**,
biological control, **barriers**, and **traps** instead. Only resort to
the use of **natural insecticides**, such as **derris**, if all else fails.

Paraquat a **contact herbicide** that will kill any plant; it is
often applied as **spot treatment** on **paths** and around the
edges of **flower**beds. Paraquat is highly poisonous and, if
ingested, may be fatal. It has no known antidote. Toxic
effects, including fatal poisoning, may also occur following
absorption through the skin. Inhalation of paraquat mist
in a confined space is thought to cause a chronic form of
poisoning, known as "paraquat lung", and it has been
withdrawn in Denmark partly because of this risk.
Paraquat is an eye and skin **irritant**, and a suspected **mutagen** and **teratogen**. It is poisonous to animals, and is thought
to be a major cause of the decline of **hares** in Britain. Its
by-products are believed to remain in the **soil** indefinitely
as pollutants, and West Germany withdrew paraquat in
1984 because of its **persistence**.

Paraquat has been listed as one of the **Dirty Dozen
Pesticides** by the International Pesticides Action Network
(see Useful Addresses, pp. 190-1). It is now banned in
Finland, USSR, Sweden, and the Netherlands, and has

been withdrawn voluntarily in Norway. Try hand **weeding**, **hoeing**, forking, or apply a **mulch** instead.

Parasite a creature or plant that lives in, or on, another creature or plant, using it as a source of food. Parasites may or may not kill the host organism. In the garden, you should encourage the ones which kill **pests**. The **ichneumon fly**, which parasitizes large white butterfly **caterpillars** is a good example. Other parasites of garden pests are available as forms of **biological control**.

Parasitic wasp the type of wasp that lays its eggs inside the bodies of a host animal or plant; a large number of wasp species are parasitic. Some inject their eggs into the bodies of **caterpillars**. Once hatched, the larvae grow, feeding first on non-essential parts of their host's body, then eating vital organs, and finally pupating in the corpse. Other species parasitize plants, usually forming **galls**.

Some parasitic wasps are a useful form of **biological control** in that they attack **pest** species. Encourage them by growing **attractant plants**, but avoid using **natural insecticides**, unless absolutely necessary, since you can kill the wasps by doing so. One parasitic wasp in particular, *Encarsia formosa*, parasitizes the glasshouse **whitefly** and is available commercially for use in the **greenhouse**.

Parsnip canker a **disease** caused by several types of **canker** fungi, which infects **parsnips** in the **soil**, usually causing orangey brown or purply black rots. Sometimes, these rots start in wounds left by **carrot fly**. To prevent canker, grow **resistant varieties** of parsnip. Sow later, at close spacing, to get small roots, which are less prone to the disease. Ensure good **drainage** and use a four year **rotation** of crops. See **Carrot fly** for control measures.

Parsnips see **Root crops**.

Paths important features in any garden, providing access from the house and linking different areas. Most garden paths are made out of concrete, paving slabs, or gravel, but if you are laying a new path, consider reusing materials. Old bricks, for example, can make an attractive path, while shredded **bark** is a good temporary pathing material, which you can use afterward as a **mulch**. You can also lay paths with brushwood. In the latter case, lay some **carpet** underneath to stop **weed** growth.

A few plants growing on paths can look very attractive, for example, hardy species, such as creeping thymes or wild **strawberries**. Remove **weeds** and grass by hand **weeding** or **flameweeding**. Keep enough of the path free of vegetation to ensure that it does not become slippery.

PCP see **Pentachlorphenol**.

Pea and bean weevils small grey or brown weevils, which are common **pests** of **peas** and broad **beans**. They chew semi-circular pieces out of the leaves, leaving an easily recognizable scalloped edge. This is not usually harmful to large plants, but you should encourage young plants to grow strongly so that they can sustain the damage. Raise them in the **greenhouse**, if necessary.

Peach a small **fruit** tree, which is best suited to a warm climate. In cooler regions, you can grow them as fans against a south-facing **wall** or in a **greenhouse**. Good **drainage** is essential. Peaches are self-fertile, so you only need one tree for **pollination**, and dwarfing **rootstocks** are not necessary because they do not grow vigorously. The main problems are **peach leaf curl** and **red spider mite**.

Peach leaf curl a common **disease** of **peaches**, almonds, and nectarines, causing puckering and reddening of the leaves. Repeated, severe attacks can weaken the **trees**. The leaf curl **fungi** overwinter on the bark of the tree and spread to young leaves during cold, wet spells in spring. Avoid growing peaches in cool, damp places. Protect **wall**-trained specimens by covering them with a temporary **polythene** shelter from the end of December to late May, the critical period when infection is most likely. Collect and burn affected leaves early in the season to prevent overwintering spores from developing.

Pea moth a small, inconspicuous moth, whose larvae are a troublesome **pest** of **pea** crops. The moth lays its eggs in June and July on pea plants that are in flower. The small **caterpillars** that emerge eat their way into pea pods and feed on the peas before pupating in the **soil**. To avoid attacks, choose your **sowing times** carefully, so that no peas are in flower when the moth is laying. Alternatively, cover flowering peas with a small mesh **netting**. Dig infected plots in winter to expose the pupae.

Pear a **fruit** tree that crops and keeps over a shorter period than **apples**. However, the gardener has a wider choice of **varieties**. In a small garden, you can train pear trees against a **wall** or **fencing**. They require warmer conditions than apples, and the blossom is susceptible to early **frosts**.

There is a choice of two **rootstocks**, the semi-dwarfing type being suitable for most varieties on most **soils**. Some pears are self-fertile, but all produce better crops following **pollination** by another **variety**, so check the pollination group of trees before buying them. The main **pests** of pears are **aphids**, **winter moth**, and **wasps**; troublesome **diseases** include **apple and pear canker**, **brown rot**, and **fireblight**.

Pear canker see **Apple and pear canker**.

Peas a hardy **vegetable**, worth eating freshly picked for the superior taste of the pods. Peas are **legumes** which fix **nitrogen** and you should grow them with **beans** in your crop **rotation**. They like a soil rich in **organic matter** and a sunny or lightly shaded site. Semi-leafless varieties need less support and are useful for growing in a **bed system**. **Pests** include **mice**, **pea moth**, and **pea and bean weevils**. Peas are also affected by **mildew**, but look out for **resistant varieties**.

Peat a deposit of saturated, semi-rotted plant remains. In the UK, peat is widely used as a **compost** material and soil conditioner. It is often sold to gardeners in bags, which are used directly for growing plants, especially acid-loving species. However, the digging of it in Britain is destroying plant and wildlife communities, and placing the continued existence of peat bogs under threat. Several conservation organizations have joined forces to try and halt peat cutting, and persuade gardeners to try other genuinely **eco-friendly** alternatives.

Compost, well-rotted **manure**, and other forms of **organic matter** can replace use of peat on beds, and fine soil mixed with well-rotted **compost** or **leafmould** should suffice for seedbeds. There are a variety of organic alternatives to peat for use in **potting composts**, including **worm compost**, leafmould, and shredded **bark** (see **Potting compost** recipes).

Pentachlorphenol (PCP) a **herbicide, fungicide,** and **insecticide** available only in mixtures, for example, with bromacil; it is also used in its pure form as a **wood preservative**. PCP is poisonous when swallowed, inhaled, or absorbed through the skin, and is an eye, skin, and respiratory system **irritant**. There is evidence that it or its contaminants are **carcinogens**. After use on turf, humans are required to stay out of an area for at least two weeks. PCP will kill all plants, including **trees**, even if only their roots extend into the treated area. There are far safer alternatives for **clearing ground**, and **cultural control** can counter pests and fungal attack. See also **biological control**, **barriers**, and **traps**.

Pentachlorphenol is extremely hazardous when used as a wood preservative, and toxic effects may be experienced some time after application. In the UK in 1990, an all-party group of MPs made an unsuccessful attempt to get PCP banned after a series of health scares. See **Timber treatment** for safer methods of treating wood.

Pentachlor-
phenol
Pepper
Permaculture
Permethrin

Pepper a half-hardy plant grown for its fruit, which is green when immature, but ripens to red, orange, yellow, or purple. In cool areas, grow peppers in a **greenhouse** or under **cloches**. Keep them with **tomatoes** in a **rotation**. **Slugs**, **aphids**, and **red spider mites** are their main **pests**.

Permaculture a new philosophy of farming and gardening, first devised in Australia, which aims for self-sufficiency on an area of land. It harmonizes organic food growing with forestry and livestock rearing, incorporating a far greater **diversity** of crops than is usual at present. Individual elements are positioned so that they are not only able to express their natural functions but also to fulfill the needs of other elements. For example, a fish **pond** in a **greenhouse** helps to keep the air humid, while the fish benefit from the extra warmth and may feed on **kitchen waste**. Each permaculture system is unique and devised to suit an individual situation – contact the Permaculture Association (see Useful Addresses, pp. 190-1) for advice. Complete permaculture is probably not possible on a back-garden scale, but you can adapt many of the techniques and design ideas to good effect.

Permethrin a **contact insecticide** of the **pyrethroid** group, used against a wide range of **pests**. Although currently popular

as a "safe" **pesticide**, it is a poison and the Nordic Expert
Group has identified it as a powerful skin and respiratory
system **irritant**. Far more controversial are claims that permethrin is a **carcinogen**. However, evidence of its being
oncogenic and a carcinogen does exist. It is toxic to **bees**
and fish, but has low mammalian toxicity and is recommended for use as a **wood preservative** with **bats**. Try **cultural
control**, **biological control**, **barriers**, and **traps** instead. Only
resort to **natural insecticides**, such as **derris**, if all else fails.

Persistence the length of time that a **pesticide** remains
active, whether in the **soil** or as a **residue** on plants. Some
of the most persistent pesticides have now been banned,
but many of those still in use remain dangerous for
months or even years. Land treated with pesticides or
artificial **fertilizers** needs to be left for at least two years
before it can be regarded as fully organic.

Persistent see **Persistence**.

Pest in the gardening sense, any animal which damages
food or ornamental plants. So-called "pests" have roles to
play in the overall balance of nature and only become a
problem in the garden because plants of the same species
are often planted together, thus providing ideal conditions
for crop-specific pests to multiply. See also **Pest control**.

Pest and disease control see **Pest control** and **Disease control**.

Pest control any measure taken to prevent damage to food
and ornamental crops from animal **pests**. In conventional
gardening, it is common practice to tackle pest problems
with chemical **pesticides**. These are unacceptable in **organic
gardening** because of the environmental and health hazards
associated with them, and a great deal of practical
research has gone into pest-control methods which do not
rely on poisons, such as **biological control**, **cultural control**,
traps, and **barriers**. To employ these methods effectively,
however, you need first to familiarize yourself with the life
cycle and **ecology** of different pests and their **natural predators**. See also **Integrated Pest Management**.

Pesticides chemical substances used to destroy animal
pests, to counter or prevent **disease**, or to kill **weeds**. These

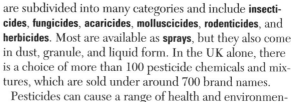

are subdivided into many categories and include **insecticides**, **fungicides**, **acaricides**, **molluscicides**, **rodenticides**, and **herbicides**. Most are available as **sprays**, but they also come in dust, granule, and liquid form. In the UK alone, there is a choice of more than 100 pesticide chemicals and mixtures, which are sold under around 700 brand names.

Pesticides can cause a range of health and environmental effects. Between 30 and 40 of them are suspected **carcinogens** and/or **teratogens** and many have been banned or restricted in other countries. A large number of pesticides are poisons, **irritants**, and/or have long-term health implications. Most damage beneficial plants and/or animals as well as pests and some can leave potentially harmful **residues** on plants and in the **soil**.

Oxfam calculates that 10,000 people a year die from pesticide poisoning worldwide, mostly in developing countries. In 1983, the World Health Organisation estimated an annual overall global figure of two million pesticide poisonings, including 4,000 fatalities. Whatever the precise figure, the death toll is admitted to be very high.

Information on health and safety hazards of different pesticides is given under individual chemical names in this book. These chemicals will be listed on the pesticide label but, in most cases, are different to the brand name.

Pest resistance
pH
Phacelia

Pest resistance see **Resistance, pest**.

pH the scale by which soil acidity is measured and which is generally an indication of how much **lime** it contains. The scale ranges from 0 to 14, with a **neutral soil** having a pH of 7.0, an **acid soil** a pH below 7.0, and an **alkaline** (limey) **soil** a pH above 7.0. The change from one pH level up to the next indicates a soil that is 10 times more alkaline. The pH is important because it influences the **soil fertility**, the range of plants that you can grow, and the severity of some **diseases**. For most purposes, the ideal value is around 6.5. You can purchase a **soil-testing** kit to measure the pH, or send a sample away for analysis.

Phacelia an annual **green manure** and a pretty **attractant plant**, *Phacelia tanacetifolia*. For use as a green manure, sow it in spring and summer. Dig it in after six to eight weeks, at any time before it flowers. If sown in late summer, it may survive a mild winter (see **Green manures** chart, pp. 80-1). It will fit anywhere in a **rotation**. In the **flower** border, its bright blue flowers will attract **beneficial insects** and **bees**.

Phosphate a constituent of many artificial **fertilizers**, which provides plants with the **phosphorus** that they need for growth. **Leaching** of phosphate can occur and contaminate water, where it may promote **algal** blooms, leading to subsequent oxygen deprivation. It is safer to add **phosphorus** in a less soluble form, so that it is released more slowly in line with the needs of plants. Many **soils** have adequate levels of phosphorus, and regular use of **manure**, **compost**, and **green manures** is sufficient to replenish stocks. If your soil is deficient in phosphorus, use the **rock fertilizer**, rock phosphate, or **bone meal** to raise levels.

Phosphorus an essential plant **nutrient**, occurring naturally in compounds, but usually provided in the form of **phosphate fertilizers**. Large quantities are needed, especially for root growth.

Phoxim an **insecticide** of the **organophosphorus** group, sold as an **ant killer**. It is moderately toxic, and harmful to **bees**. For safer, alternative methods of control, see **Ants**.

Phytoseiulus persimilis a predatory mite, which you can introduce into the **greenhouse** as a **biological control** for **red spider mite**. *Phytoseiulus persimilis* catches and eats its prey, but does no harm to any other creature. It is sold through the post, either on leaf sections or in a bottle of bran. Introduce this control as soon as you see the first red spider mites in spring: do not let numbers build up.

Picloram a **translocated herbicide**, used either alone or in mixtures with **2,4-D** or bromacil, for **weed control** on grass. It is an eye, skin, and respiratory system **irritant** and there is evidence that it is an animal **carcinogen**. Picloram has a long **persistence** and can remain in dead plant material in toxic amounts. It is harmful to fish, and there is a high risk of **spray drift** damage. Use of picloram is restricted in the USA, and banned in Finland and Sweden. Try hand **weeding**, **hoeing**, or apply a **mulch**.

Piperonyl butoxide a synergistic chemical added to **pyrethroid** and related **pesticides** to increase their effectiveness. ▷

Phosphate
Phosphorus
Phoxim
Phytoseiulus persimilis
Picloram
Piperonyl butoxide

Although not particularly poisonous, piperonyl butoxide can increase your sensitivity to other toxic substances. Most **pyrethrum** insecticides have piperonyl butoxide added, and so are not suitable for use in **organic gardening**.

Pirimicarb an **insecticide** of the **carbamate** group, used in a variety of forms against **aphids**. It is a poison, an **anticholinesterase** compound, and, in its concentrated form, an eye and skin **irritant**. Pirimicarb is harmful to animals and has a **harvest interval** of up to two weeks.

Pirimiphos methyl an **insecticide** of the **organophosphorus** group, used on **fruit**, **vegetables**, and stored grain. It is mildly poisonous, an eye and skin **irritant**, and an **anticholinesterase** compound. Evidence exists that it is a potential **mutagen**. It is **persistent**, with a **harvest interval** ranging from three days to three weeks, and is dangerous to **bees** and fish. Try **cultural control**, **biological control**, **traps**, and **barriers** instead. Only resort to the use of **natural insecticides**, such as **derris**, if all else fails.

Planting times see **Sowing times**.

Plant raising a method of growing your own plants from seed or **cuttings**. It enables you to grow plants organically from the start and to look after them well so that they will be both vigorous and healthy when you transplant them. Raising plants yourself is usually better than accepting them from neighbours or buying them, since there is less risk of introducing **pests** and **diseases** into the garden. Plants propagated from **cuttings** or runners, or by dividing a large plant, will inherit any **virus** diseases of the parent plant. It is thus best not to propagate susceptible plants, such as **strawberries** and other soft **fruit**, unless you are sure they are healthy.

Plant spacing the distance at which you place a plant apart from its neighbour. This is determined by the amount of food, moisture, and space that it needs in order to grow to the size that you require. Wide rows of **vegetable** crops are usually wasteful. You can make better use of light, air, and **soil** resources, which are evenly distributed, by positioning plants equal distances apart on a **bed system**. The spacing of most vegetable crops not only affects the total yield but the size of the individual plants, and thus should depend on how big you want them to grow. For example, widely spaced **onions**, 22cm (9in) apart each way, will give you large bulbs, but fewer of them. A closer spacing of 10cm (4in) will give you a higher yield of medium-sized bulbs. Much closer than this and the yield will start to decline, in addition to the bulbs getting smaller.

Plastic a durable, synthetic material, which is used in the manufacture of garden **tools**, for covering **greenhouses** and other garden structures, and for **clearing ground** prior to cultivation. Plastics are currently made from oil, a non-renewable resource, and have severe disposal problems. Most so-called "**biodegradable**" plastics do not fully decompose, but simply break up into tiny particles which remain in the **soil** indefinitely; many plastics also give off toxic fumes if burnt. If you do buy garden tools or containers made from plastic, make sure they are strong enough to last; for tool handles, wood is usually preferable. When covering greenhouses or **cloches**, choose plastic designed for the purpose; other types will only last about five years, and few more than ten, unless kept out of direct sunlight. In general, plastic is an ideal material for rendering structures watertight and/or durable, and, in the form of black **polythene**, is also extremely effective for clearing ground of **weeds**, because it deprives them of light. However, avoid using plastic in any form for situations where it is intended to decompose, for example, as a long-term **mulch**. In the UK, there are a few recycling points run by local authorities, but these will only take some types of plastic.

Plastic
Plum

Plum a **fruit** tree, which is less adaptable than **apples** or **pears**, and not always a reliable cropper. Plums will grow as fans on the semi-dwarfing **rootstock** "Pixie", and if allowed to form a bush on this rootstock will make an attractive specimen in a larger garden. Most varieties are self-fertile and do not require **pollination**. Plums flower early, and may lose blossom to **frost**. Some of the fine dessert varieties flourish only in warm regions or against a south wall, but cooking varieties are more tolerant. Damsons are hardier than plums and make useful trees in a shelter belt. The main **disease** of plums is **silverleaf**, but **brown rot** may also be a problem. **Pests** include **aphids**, **wasps**, and **birds**.

133

Plum sawfly see **Sawfly**.

Poached-egg plant a low-growing hardy annual, *Limnanthes douglasii*, which is a good **attractant plant**, especially for **hoverflies**, and is also loved by **bees**. It grows best on a sunny site, and will self-seed.

Pollination the transfer of pollen from the male to the female parts of a flower resulting in fertilization or "setting", and the development of seed or fruit. Pollination is usually carried out by **bees** or other insects or by the wind, but some plants will pollinate themselves without help.

Pollination is not usually a problem with **vegetable** crops. Tomatoes grown in **greenhouses** sometimes benefit if you shake them lightly to help the fruit set. Runner beans may not set well in very hot weather – a failure often wrongly blamed on bumble bees or pollen beetles.

If you are growing crops for **seed saving**, you need to know which crops are self-pollinating and therefore can be grown together without crossing, for example, **lettuce** and **tomatoes**, and also which ones need isolating.

Pollination is an important consideration when choosing **fruit** trees. Some, such as **peaches** and certain **plums**, are self-pollinating. However, most other fruit trees benefit from being near to another variety bearing the same fruit and one which flowers at the same time, so that the two can pollinate each other. Otherwise, there may be no fruit or much reduced yields. Varieties of plums, **apples**, and **pears** are divided into "pollination groups" according to when they flower: those appearing in the same or adjacent groups are able to pollinate each other. Check the pollination groups of fruit trees before you buy them.

Pollution see **Air pollution** and **Water pollution**.

Polythene a type of **plastic**, with many uses in the garden. Black polythene is particularly effective for **clearing ground** of **weeds** because it excludes light.

Pond a valuable element of **nature gardening**, in that it can form a refuge for threatened species, such as **frogs**, **toads**, and **newts**, which are useful **natural predators**. To make a garden pond, simply dig a hole of the size you want, but bear in mind that it should be at least 60cm (2ft) deep if you want to keep fish or creatures that will overwinter in the pond. You will need a shallower area for spawning and for pond creatures that need more sunlight. Varying the depths also enables you to grow a wider variety of plants. In at least one place along the bank, create a slope or install a plank so that amphibians can crawl in and out.

To make the pond watertight, either buy a ready-made liner or make one of your own from concrete, black **plastic**, or rubber. Concrete has a tendency to crack, and needs to be left filled with standing water for some time before anything much can live in it. Black plastic is cheaper, but only lasts a few years. Butyl rubber is probably best. Remove any sharp stones and put down a layer of sand and **newspaper** or old **carpet** to minimize risk of puncturing. Then, lay the rubber, and fill it with water. Allow the weight of the water to ease the rubber into the pond's contours before securing it with rocks at the edge.

Once installed, you can introduce species native to Britain, such as sticklebacks. Many pond-living creatures will arrive on their own in due course, but by adding a little water and sediment from a mature pond, you can introduce a range of species at an early stage. Bear in mind that fish will eat frog or toad spawn. If your pond becomes clogged with filamentous algae, pull most of it out and introduce plants with large, floating leaves, which will reduce the amount of sunlight and **nutrients** available, and slow algal growth.

Potassium

Potassium permanganate

Potassium an essential **nutrient** for plant growth, required in large amounts and particularly associated with the size and quality of **fruit**. Most **soils** contain good supplies of potassium, but it is often "locked up" and not readily available to plants. Encouraging the activity of **microorganisms** in the soil by applying **compost** and other forms of **organic matter**, and using **green manures** in a **rotation**, is the best way of increasing supplies of potassium over the long term. For more immediate effect, use **comfrey**, animal **manures**, or **seaweed meal**, which are good sources of potassium. A light **sandy soil** may be deficient in potassium: correct this by using the **rock fertiizer**, rock potash.

Potassium permanganate an **insecticide**, used on a range of **pests**. It is a poison. It has no additional long-term health effects as far as is known.

Potato a **vegetable**, cultivated for its edible tuber. If you have no room for a main crop of potatoes, try growing early **varieties** that you can eat freshly dug, and perhaps a few salad potatoes. The crop needs a sunny site and a **soil** rich in **organic matter**. Potatoes belong to the Solanaceae family, and should be kept with **tomatoes** in your crop **rotation**. Avoid adding **lime** to this plot in the rotation for as long as possible before planting, since an **alkaline soil** will encourage **scab**, a common **disease** of potatoes. Start by buying seed tubers that have been certified free from disease. Tubers are traditionally planted in widely spaced rows of trenches, allowing you to earth up the plants. On a **bed system**, put the tubers in with a trowel at equidistant spacing, and apply an organic **mulch**, such as **hay**, while they are growing. In a no-dig system, place the tubers directly on the **soil** surface with a mulch on top. Avoid a light-coloured mulch in cold regions since this increases the risk of **frost** damage. A most troublesome disease is **potato and tomato blight**, which can cause severe losses in an organic garden. Choose less susceptible varieties, where possible. Other problems include common **scab**, **potato blackleg**, **slugs**, **wireworms**, and **eelworms**.

Potato
Potato and tomato blight

Potato and tomato blight a common **disease**, serious in wet areas. On **potatoes**, the first symptoms are brown blotches on the leaves, often at the tips and edges; a white mould may appear beneath the blotches on the underside of the leaves. The disease does not normally appear until June, but then spreads rapidly in warm, humid conditions, over 60°F (16°C), and can destroy all the foliage. The tubers develop brown lesions and gradually rot.

On **tomatoes**, the disease causes similar symptoms on the leaves and hard brown patches on green fruit. Ripe fruit rots rapidly. In areas where blight is a problem, you can grow tomatoes in a **greenhouse** where they will be protected and less likely to get infected.

With potatoes, use **varieties** that are less susceptible, and buy certified seed tubers. Earth up tubers or **mulch** them to reduce the number of spores that might be washed on to them if plants become infected. However, once symptoms appear on the leaves, there is little you can do, except to cut off the leaves and **compost** them, and wait for at least three weeks before digging the tubers. Where blight is a problem, grow only early maturing varieties

136

that are harvestable by the time attacks occur. Remove all tubers and crop debris at the end of the season.

Potato blackleg a common **disease** of potatoes. On infected plants, the first symptoms are often yellowing upper leaves caused by the stems rotting just above the base. Tubers may then rot while in the ground, or in store. The disease is spread in tubers or in plant debris. Grow less susceptible **varieties**, ensure good **drainage**, and use a **rotation**. Make sure all tubers and debris are removed at harvest time. Check stored potatoes for signs of rot.

Potato cyst eelworm see **Eelworm**.

Potato scab see **Scab**.

Potato blackleg

Potato cyst eelworm

Potato scab

Potting composts

Potting composts mixtures for growing plants in containers, which you can either buy or make yourself. Potting composts must contain sufficient plant **nutrients**, and also retain air and moisture when packed into a pot. Many of those on the market contain chemical **fertilizers** and **peat**, but you can buy organic ones, usually based on **worm compost** or composted **farmyard manure**. Various substances are being tried out by compost manufacturers as alternatives to peat, so look out for potting composts containing ecologically sound materials, such as **straw** or shredded **bark**.

Possible ingredients for home-made potting composts include **leafmould**, sterilized loam, garden **compost**, **worm compost**, and **natural fertilizers** such as **seaweed meal** and **bone meal** (see recipes below). Check the **pH** of your compost and add **lime** or **calcified seaweed** as necessary. Experiment to find one suited to your plants and growing conditions.

Home-Made Potting Compost Recipes

Recipe 1	Recipe 2
1 part loam	4 parts loam
2 parts compost from **compost heap** or **wormbin**	2 parts leafmould
1 part fine grade bark or **leafmould**	**plus for every 54.5l (12gal) of mixture:**
	225g (8oz) of seaweed meal
	112g (4oz) of bone meal
	56g (2oz) of calcified seaweed

Poultry manure a useful **natural fertilizer**, which is rich in **nitrogen** and works best if mixed with plant debris and made into **compost**. It is possible to buy in poultry manure, but avoid that produced by battery systems, both because of ethical considerations and because some of the additives used in animal feeds may be passed out in the faeces. The best option of all is to keep chickens yourself. If you have a mobile run, some of their manure will go straight into the **soil**, and you can collect the rest together with the bedding straw for adding to the **compost heap**.

Propachlor a soil-acting **herbicide**, used against germinating **weeds** around **brassicas**, **onions**, **leeks**, **strawberries**, and ornamental plants. It is a poison, which can be absorbed through the skin and may cause sensitization on contact. It has some cumulative toxicity, and is particularly hazardous at high temperatures. Propachlor is an eye and skin **irritant**, and has been identified as a potential **mutagen** and **teratogen**. The US National Institute for Occupational Safety and Health records severe skin reactions following use of this chemical. Propachlor is toxic to fish. Try hand **weeding**, **hoeing**, or apply a **mulch** instead.

Propagation see **Plant raising**.

Propiconazole a **systemic fungicide** used against **mildew** and **rust**. It is most commonly used on grain crops, although there are some garden formulations available. It is a mild poison and an eye and skin **irritant**, with a **harvest interval** of at least four weeks on cereals crops. Propiconazole is hazardous to fish. See **Mildew, powdery**, **Mildew, downy**, and **Rust** for specific control measures.

Propoxur an **insecticide** of the **carbamate** group used against a range of **pests**, and available as a **fumigant** for **greenhouse** use. It is a poison, an **anticholinesterase** product, and an eye and respiratory system **irritant**. There is evidence that it may be a **mutagen** and that both it and its breakdown products may affect the reproductive system. It is harmful to **birds**, wildlife, and to fish, and can damage some plants. Try **cultural control**, **biological control**, **traps**, and **barriers** instead. Only resort to the use of **natural insecticides**, such as **derris**, if all else fails.

Protective clothing any form of clothing used to protect humans against the potentially harmful effects of **pesticides**. At the least, this means trousers, a long-sleeved shirt or coat, and gloves, but in many cases, a mask and respirator are also necessary. Protective clothing should be stored separately, and not used for any other function. Although garden pesticides are supposed to be formulated in such weak solutions that full protective clothing is unnecessary, an increasing number of pesticide users do wear it, especially when dealing with **irritant sprays**. For professional applications, full protective suits are worn. Protective clothing cannot provide complete protection and **spray drift** can penetrate many fabrics.

Pruning the practice of cutting back woody plants. You may need to prune **trees** and **shrubs** for several reasons: to train them into shape; to limit their growth; to encourage fruiting or flowering; or to control **pests** and **diseases**. Fruit **trees** and bushes, especially trained forms such as espaliers, need regular, careful pruning. In general, prune in summer to restrict growth and to encourage fruiting, and prune in winter to encourage and train new growth. Many ornamental trees and shrubs need little pruning, although there are exceptions, for example, bush roses.

Pruning to remove dead and diseased wood is an important part of garden **hygiene** and helps to control diseases, such as **apple and pear canker** and **silver leaf**. It can also effectively remove pests. Summer pruning of gooseberry bushes, for example, involves removing most of the young growing tips where **aphids** usually congregate.

Most pruning wounds heal quickly without the help of any artificial sealant. However, where there is a risk of infection, the timing of pruning can be critical. For example, you should not prune **plums** in winter because of the risk of silver leaf infection.

Pumpkins see **Squashes**.

PVC abbreviation of polyvinyl chloride, a **plastic** used as a building material and in packaging. PVC releases toxic fumes when burnt, so avoid putting it on a **bonfire**.

Pyracantha a prickly evergreen **shrub** of the genus *Pyracantha*, which you can grow as a bush, trained against a **wall**, or as a **hedge**. All species have white flowers, loved by **bees**, followed by red, orange, or yellow berries. Most of the berries attract **birds**. Pyracanthas grow well in most garden **soils**, either in sun or partial shade. **Fireblight** and **scab** may be troublesome, although there are varieties that are **resistant** to the latter.

Pyrethroids a class of synthetic **pesticides**. Pyrethroids are chemically similar to the **natural insecticide, pyrethrum**. They are, on the whole, safer than traditional **organochlorine**, **organophosphorus**, and **carbamate pesticides**, but some still pose health risks, or are under suspicion of doing so. There is, for example, evidence that **permethrin** is a **carcinogen**. In addition, there are increasing instances of pest **resistance** to pyrethroids, and it is feared that this may be transferred to pyrethrum. For these reasons, pyrethroids are not used in **organic gardening**.

Pyrethroids
Pyrethrum

Pyrethrum a **natural insecticide** that is present naturally in the flowers of *Pyrethrum cineraefolium,* from which it is extracted for garden use. Despite its adoption by the organic movement, it is a poison and a potential **allergen** and/or **irritant**. Its advantages are its low mammalian toxicity and very short **persistence**: by spraying in the evening or on dull days, for example, you can virtually eliminate any risk to **bees**. It is often used in combination with the stronger, and potentially more toxic, natural insecticide, **derris**. Unfortunately, most commercially available pyrethrum formulations also contain the catalyst **piperonyl butoxide**, making them unacceptable to organic gardeners. Try **cultural control**, **biological control**, **traps**, and **barriers**. Only resort to derris or **insecticidal soap** if all else fails.

Quassia a **natural insecticide**, mainly extracted from the tropical quassia tree. Quassia is one of the few insecticides approved of by organic gardeners, although its use is illegal in Britain at present because it has not been officially registered. Quassia is mildly poisonous to humans. It has no additional long-term health effects.

Quintozene a **fungicide** applied as a dust against **damping off** in **fruit**, **vegetables**, and **flowers**, and also as a **spray** on **lawns**. It is an eye and skin **irritant** and has been identified as a possible **carcinogen** and **mutagen**. Its toxicity level rises when oil is used as the spraying medium. In the past, quintozene formulations contained toxic contaminants, which are thought to have been animal **teratogens**.

Quintozene has a long **persistence** and can do damage to members of the **cucumber** family planted in treated **soil**, and also to **tomatoes** grown in **compost** made from treated materials. At least four pathogens have shown **resistance** to this chemical. Try **cultural control** instead.

Rabbit when wild, a **pest** if it invades your garden and capable of wreaking havoc among **vegetable** crops and ornamentals. The best way to keep wild rabbits out is to put up close-mesh **fencing**, buried at least 30cm (12in) into the soil and curving outward to dissuade them from burrowing. You can also buy **electric fences** that are specially designed for the purpose.

141

Radish a quick-growing salad plant, useful for **intercropping** between other **vegetables**. Winter and mooli radishes grow much slower and produce larger edible roots than other **varieties**. Keep them with **brassicas** in your crop **rotation**. Radishes do best in well-drained, moist **soil**. In summer, sow them in light shade. The main **pests** are **fleabeetles** and **cabbage root flies**.

Raised beds a system of growing on beds raised above ground level, which is useful on heavy **soils** for improving **drainage**; it also helps the soil warm up in spring. In a **bed system**, raising the level of the soil occurs naturally as you cultivate and add **organic matter**. However, you can also construct higher raised beds by building a framework of **timber** or brick around the proposed planting area, and adding extra soil and **organic matter**.

Raspberries see **Cane fruit**.

Raspberry beetle a small beetle, whose larvae are common **pests** of all **cane fruit**. The tiny maggots tunnel into ripening berries, where you will often find them when picking. In winter, lightly cultivate the **soil** near canes that have been affected to expose the pupae. As a last resort, spray with **derris** as soon as flowering has finished.

Rat a surprisingly frequent garden dweller, and one to be wary of because of the high incidence of disease among rats in general, in particular the potentially fatal Weill's Disease. The bacteria *Leptospirum* that causes the disease is carried in rats' **urine** and requires moisture to survive, but recently there have been fears that it can persist in **compost** material. You can cut down on the risks of infection by always wearing protective gloves when handling compost and by disinfecting and covering any cuts. To make your **compost heap** less attractive to rats, avoid putting cooked food scraps, such as meat and cheese, on the heap. Alternatively, use a **tumbler** rather than a compost heap or buy a rat-proof **compost bin**.

Getting rid of rats is a problem unless you own a cat which is a skilled and fierce hunter. Anti-coagulant **rodenticides** are an inhumane way to kill rodents, causing them to die slowly from bleeding and dehydration; they are also potentially lethal to humans and other animals. Trapping results in a quicker death without the risks associated with poison, but it is a highly skilled process. There are rat traps available for home use but these are quite dangerous to use and can easily break fingers. In any case, rats are intelligent and often avoid them anyway. In the UK, most local authorities have rodent-control officers, who can offer specialist advice. If you allow them to deal with the problem for you, you should be aware that they will employ the most effective poison with little regard for its toxicity. Make sure that any poison used is well hidden from children and from other animals, and in a container so it can be safely disposed of later on.

Rat and mouse poison see **Rodenticide**.

Recycling the practice of breaking down **waste** material into its constituent parts for use again in a different form. Recycling is central to **organic gardening** practice – biodegradable materials are either added to the **compost heap** to form **organic matter**, or applied directly to the **soil** where they gradually break down and provide plant **nutrients**. In addition to recycling, you can reuse many household products in the garden: pop bottles can make good **bottle cloches**; various household containers can serve as flower pots; and old **carpets** provide a **weed**-suppressing underlay for **paths** and also help to keep **compost** warm. Note that it takes **energy** and resources to recycle something, so that it is almost always preferable to reuse it.

Redcurrants see **Bush fruit**.

Red spider mite a spider-like mite, of which two species are particularly troublesome **pests**. Glasshouse red spider mites cause speckling and bronzing of plant leaves, and if their numbers are allowed to increase, they may form a fine silk webbing. They attack many plants in **greenhouses**, and also, sometimes, certain garden plants, particularly when it is hot and dry. **Strawberries** are commonly affected. The simplest way to prevent this pest in the greenhouse is to keep the atmosphere humid and to spray susceptible plants regularly with a fine mist of water. **Hygiene** is also important. Cut off the old leaves of strawberries after fruiting, and clear away plant debris and old **mulch**. Wash down greenhouses in winter to destroy hibernating mites.

Encourage richness and diversity when creating your own nature garden.

Native trees and shrubs To cater for the **birds**, choose species with winter berries as well as those with dense summer foliage for nest cover. Certain native **trees** can house as many as 200 different insect species.

Wall covered with ivy or other creeper Climbing plants provide nesting spaces for small birds. Insects love the nectar of mature **ivy** flowers, which appear late in the year when other food is scarce.

Buddleia and other plants for butterflies More than any other plant, **buddleia** is renowned for its power to attract **butterflies**.

Bird table Choose a **bird table** with a lipped edge to prevent food falling to the ground. Birds mostly need feeding over winter months when food is scarce in the garden. Suitable scraps include nuts, grains, seeds, and coconut shells.

Nest boxes Mount **nest boxes** on trees using wire rather than nails, or **fencing**. Use hinged tops so that you can clean out old nesting material and prevent **parasites** building up.

Native plants Choose **attractant plants**, including those with single open flowerheads, to provide food for a range of **beneficial insects** and small invertebrates. Remember to include food plants for larvae as well as adults.

144

Seeding plants with heads left on
By allowing **native plants** to go to seed, you can attract seed-eating birds and create your own reservoir of **native seed**.

Wildflower meadow Either collect your own seed from local wild grasses and meadow flowers or buy a ready-prepared mix. Choose meadow species suited to your **soil type**.

Pond A garden **pond** provides a **habitat** for **frogs** and **toads**, both of which feed on **slugs**. You can introduce useful aquatic life at an early stage by adding mature pond water.

Plants for shallow and deep water
Varying the depths of your pond will enable you to plant a wider range of aquatic plants.

Escape plank for frogs and toads If you have amphibians breeding in the pond, they will need a plank or a gentle slope at the edge of the pond to help them get out of the water.

Compost bin Rotting plant material creates a suitable habitat for **worms** and **spiders**.

Wild area to attract small mammals and amphibians Valuable **natural predators** will settle only if there is an area of long grass or shrubby vegetation, left undisturbed, to provide them with cover.

Pile of old wood and stones A stack of rotting wood and stones attracts a diverse array of insects and provides nesting spaces for **mice**, **voles**, and small birds.

You can also introduce a **biological control** into the greenhouse, the predatory mite, **_Phytoseiulus persimilis_**, which feeds on the red spider mite.

The fruit tree red spider mite causes similar damage to the leaves of **apples**, **pears**, and **plums**. Encourage **natural predators**, such as **anthocorid bugs**, and avoid spraying since these **beneficial insects** are easily killed. As a last resort, use the **natural insecticide, derris**.

Residue, pesticide any trace of a **pesticide** that remains on plants or in **soil** over a period. Some pesticides leave potentially harmful residues on food plants, especially if these are harvested and eaten within the **harvest interval**. In the USA, research has indicated that some pesticide residues may be **carcinogens**. Health risks from pesticide residues are small compared to, say, those posed by cigarette smoking, but not insignificant.

Residue,
pesticide

Resistance,
pest

Resistant
variety

Resistance, pest the immunity that some **pests** develop to particular **pesticides**. If individual pests in a population are naturally resistant to a pesticide, they will tend to survive after spraying, and the offspring they produce will make up an increasingly large proportion of the overall population. If resistance is then passed on genetically between generations, it will gradually spread to the rest of the population, and the pesticide will no longer be effective.

There are hundreds of cases of pest resistance already known, and the rate at which different species develop it continues to increase.

On the whole, the more pesticides are used, the greater the chance there is of resistance occurring.

Resistant variety a **variety** of a plant that shows some **resistance** to a particular **pest** or **disease**. Plant breeders are now taking more account of this factor and new resistant varieties are being introduced all the time, particularly in the case of **vegetables** and soft **fruit**, but also with regard to some **flowers** and fruit **trees**. For instance, there are **lettuces** resistant to **root aphids**, **potatoes** resistant to **potato and tomato blight**, **gooseberries** resistant to **mildew**, and roses resistant to **blackspot**. This does not neccessarily mean that the plants are immune to the pest or disease, just that they are less susceptible. The extent of their resistance will also depend on growing conditions.

Resmethrin a non-**systemic fungicide** of the **pyrethroid** group. It is a mild **irritant**, toxic to **bees** and fish, and moderately **persistent**. Try **cultural control** instead.

Rhubarb an easy-to-grow plant cultivated for its edible leaf stalks, which are eaten as a fruit and are harvestable in spring. The temperate species is very hardy, generally trouble free, and will grow in any **soil**, provided you give it plenty of well-rotted **manure**. It likes a sunny or partially shaded site, and is handsome enough to put among **flowers** in a border. Rhubarb contains oxalic acid, which makes the stems of most varieties inedible and potentially toxic by midsummer. In the past, gardeners used the boiled-up leaves to make a **natural insecticide**.

Rock fertilizers natural rocks that are crushed and ground to a powder and used to provide the **soil** with **minerals**. Rock fertilizers remain for a long time in the soil and only very slowly release **nutrients** for plants. Thus, you can use them for long-term correction of any **mineral deficiencies** that show up in **soil testing**.

Resmethrin
Rhubarb
Rock fertilizers
Rodenticide

Two of the principal rock fertilizers are rock phosphate, used to supply **phosphorus**, and rock potash, which is a source of **potassium**. They both release nutrients very slowly, especially rock potash. In fact, many soils already contain plenty of potassium, but in a "locked-up" form, which is not available to plants and does not show up in a soil analysis. Organic practices, such as adding **organic matter** and growing **green manures**, help to release potassium for growing crops. However, if you have a light, **sandy soil**, it is more likely to be deficient in this mineral, so you should apply rock potash as a preventative measure.

Other commonly used rock fertilizers include: **gypsum**, which contains **sulphur** and **calcium**, and **dolomite**, which provides calcium and **magnesium** and raises soil **pH**.

Rodenticide a **pesticide** used for killing **rats** and **mice**. Many rodenticides are anti-coagulants, causing rats and mice to die slow deaths from bleeding and dehydration. Not only are these a cruel and inhumane method of control, but they also mean that the rat or mouse is likely to hide away somewhere inaccessible when it begins to feel ill and, once dead, will smell dreadful and pose a health risk as it decomposes. Rodenticides are also extremely hazardous to humans, in particular children, and animals. See **Rats** for safer, alternative methods of control.

Root aphids small, pale-coloured **aphids**, often covered in a white, powdery, wax-like substance. They attack plant roots, causing stunted growth; in some cases, plants will wilt and die. Pot plants, **lettuces**, primulas, and carnations are particularly susceptible. Remove infested plants, and dig over ground to expose aphids. Practising **rotation** and using **resistant varieties** of lettuce helps prevent attacks.

Root aphids
Root crops
Rooting powders
Rootstock
Rotation

Root crops any **vegetables** with swollen, edible roots. Root crops, such as carrots, parsnips, and beetroot, are best kept together in a **rotation**. They need the same growing conditions – an open site and a light, well-drained **soil** (a plot composted for a previous crop is ideal). They also suffer from many of the same soil-borne **pests** and **diseases**.

By sowing quick-maturing **varieties** of carrots in early spring, and growing a main crop for winter storage, you can have a fresh supply for most of the year. Follow the same guidelines for beetroot, but choose a bolt-resistant variety for early sowings in cold regions. Parsnips are hardy and you can grow them as a staple winter crop.

Carrots and parsnips are **umbellifers**, and share **carrot fly** as their main pest. Parsnips also suffer from **parsnip canker**, but there are some **resistant varieties.** Downy **mildew** and **scab** can both affect beetroot.

Rooting powders mixtures of chemicals, usually including **pesticides**, which increase the rate at which **cuttings** take root. These are unacceptable in **organic gardening**.

Rootstock the root system of a plant on to which another variety has been grafted. This is normally done to alter the characteristics of the resultant plant. For example, many **fruit trees** are grafted in this way to control their vigour and ultimate size, a dwarfing rootstock being suitable for a small garden with fertile **soil**. Grafting on to rootstocks is also used to propagate plants that are difficult to raise successfully by other means.

Rotation a system in which **vegetable** crops are moved to a different spot in the garden each year to avoid the build up of soil-borne **pests** and **diseases**. This also makes better

use of **soil fertility**, because different crops require different **nutrients**. Group together crops in the same family,
since these will usually suffer from the same pests and
diseases. The major groups are: **brassicas** (crops of the
cabbage family); **onion** family crops; **root crops**, together
with **celery** and other **umbellifers**; **legumes** (mostly **beans** and
peas); and **potatoes**. Allocate plots to these crops according
to your needs and the space available, planning the rotation so that a particular group does not return to its
original plot for several years. You should also consider
any other aspects of the rotated crops. For example, the
fact that legumes add **nitrogen** to the **soil** and so should be
followed by a demanding crop, such as brassicas.

Rotavating a method of turning the **soil**, involving the use
of a rotary cultivator. Rotavating can be helpful in a large
garden as a means of incorporating **organic matter** and **green
manures**, and sometimes also for **clearing ground**. However,
rotavating can damage the **soil structure** and may also create an impermeable layer, 15 to 20cm (6 to 8in) below the
surface. Thus, use a rotavator occasionally if you need to,
but not routinely. You will have to rotavate several times
over a few months to get rid of perennial **weeds**.

Rotenone another name for **Derris**.

Runner beans see **Beans**.

Rust a common **disease** caused by various **fungi**, each
attacking specific plants, or groups of plants. It commonly
shows as orange or brown pustules on leaves. A wide
range of **vegetables**, **fruit**, **trees**, and ornamental plants are
frequently affected, for example, broad **beans**, **leeks**,
onions, **plums**, antirrhinums, geraniums, hollyhocks, mint,
and roses. Rust does not always cause serious damage,
although severe attacks can both weaken plants and make
ornamentals look unsightly. Use less susceptible varieties
where available, for example, of antirrhinums, roses, and
leeks. Grow hollyhocks as annuals. Burn off the old debris
of mint in the autumn to kill any overwintering spores
present on the leaves or **soil** surface. Use a **flameweeder** to
do this or cover the plants with **straw** and set light to them.
Leek rust is encouraged by soils that are high in **nitrogen**
and low in **potassium**, or that have poor **drainage**.

Sandy soil a free-draining **soil type** which is easy to work. It warms up quickly in the spring, so you can cultivate it early. However, it also loses **nutrients** and **organic matter** quickly, and therefore requires plentiful supplies of **compost** or **manure** to keep it fertile and to help it hold water, particularly if you want to grow **vegetable** and **fruit** crops. Many attractive plants which need good **drainage**, such as shrubby, aromatic **herbs**, thrive on sandy soils.

Sawdust an organic material, for use with caution in the garden because it uses up a lot of **nitrogen** as it decomposes. For this reason, never dig fresh sawdust into the **soil**. However, in small quantities, sawdust makes a useful addition to the **compost heap**, as long as you also add nitrogen-rich materials, such as **poultry manure**. Be wary of sawdust from treated **timber** since it can contain toxic materials which may be hazardous if inhaled.

Sawfly a small, inconspicuous insect, resembling a flying **ant**, whose **caterpillar**-like larvae are damaging **pests** of several types of **fruit** and ornamental plant.
   Gooseberry sawfly larvae (see p. 17) can quickly reduce the leaves of **gooseberries** and currants to skeletons. There may be several generations of them within a single year, so inspect bushes regularly, picking off any pin-holed leaves, which you will find carry clusters of eggs and tiny larvae. As a last resort, spray with **derris**.

Apple and plum sawfly larvae burrow into the developing fruit. Pick up and **compost** all fallen fruitlets in summer to help prevent future problems.

Roses are affected by several different species of sawfly, feeding mainly on leaves. Cultivate the **soil** lightly around affected bushes in winter.

Scab, common a fungal **disease**, which is most damaging to **potatoes** but also affects **beetroots**, **radishes**, **swedes**, and **turnips**, causing spots of corky and, sometimes, pitted tissue to develop on the tubers or roots. It is most prevalent during hot, dry summers and on light, **alkaline soils**.

This disease usually has little effect on yields, but looks unsightly and makes peeling more neccessary. To reduce the likelihood of scab in potatoes, use **resistant varieties**. Do not **lime** the plot prior to planting them in a crop **rotation**; instead, add **lawn mowings** to the **soil** to make conditions more acid. Water susceptible crops in dry conditions, especially on light soil.

Potatoes are also affected by a more serious powdery scab, which can be a problem on heavy, wet soils. You can avoid this form of the disease by improving **drainage**. You should also destroy all diseased tubers and use as long a **rotation** as possible. See also **Apple scab**.

Scale insects small, sap-feeding insects and troublesome garden **pests** (see p. 17), easily recognizable because they are covered with waxy scales.

Scale insects mostly attack ornamental plants, particularly in **greenhouses**, but they also affect some **fruit**, especially **currants**, **peaches**, and vines. They can make a plant look unsightly because they excrete a sticky "honeydew", which encourages sooty moulds to grow. Bad infestations can seriously weaken plants.

Examine plants you buy carefully to avoid bringing in this pest. If ornamentals with robust leaves are affected, you can wipe the scales off using a soft cloth or brush, dipped in soapy water. As a last resort, spray affected plants with **insecticidal soap**.

Sea holly a perennial plant of the genus *Eryngium*, with thistle-like flowers. It is a good **attractant plant**, and loved by **bees**. It grows best on **sandy soils** in full sun. Most varieties are tall, from 50 to 100cm (20 to 40in) in height.

Scab, common
Scale insects
Sea holly

151

Seaweed in its fresh form, a good **natural fertilizer**, which provides useful amounts of the main plant **nutrients**, especially **potassium**, plus a whole range of other **minerals** and **trace elements**. It contains compounds called alginates, whose binding action improves the **soil structure**. Alginates also encourage the activity of **bacteria** in the **compost heap**, making seaweed a good **compost activator**. Another interesting effect of seaweed, not yet fully substantiated, is that it improves a plant's vigour, and increases its resistance to **pests** and **diseases**, and to **frost**. It is for these reasons that liquid seaweed extracts are sold as growth promoters. They do not contain sufficient nutrients to act as **liquid feeds**, but they can correct trace-element deficiencies. Use them as a foliar **spray** or water them on to the **soil**.

Seaweed is sometimes polluted by radioactivity or other industrial effluent, so check whether your coast is likely to be affected before collecting it. The Marine Conservation Society (see Useful Addresses, pp. 190-1) publishes a guide to Britain's beaches with respect to pollution. Do not remove seaweed from where it is growing or you will damage the fragile shore **ecology**. You can collect odd pieces left lying on the shore after a storm, but do so only in moderation since the drift line too has an interesting and vulnerable ecology.

Seaweed
Seaweed meal
Seed composts

Seaweed meal a ground, dried form of **seaweed**, which is sold mainly as a **natural fertilizer**. It contains **nitrogen** and **potassium** and a whole range of **trace elements** in a fairly slowly released form. Like fresh seaweed, it is a good soil conditioner and an effective **compost activator**.

Seed composts mixtures for sowing seeds in pots or trays that you can buy or make yourself. Seed composts do not contain many plant **nutrients**, so you must prick out the seedlings as soon as they are big enough into a richer **potting compost**. Off-the-shelf "multipurpose", or "seed and potting", composts contain more nutrients than ordinary seed composts and are designed both for sowing and growing-on plants. Most seed composts on the market contain chemical **fertilizers** and **peat**, but there are some organic and peat-free ones available. You can also try making your own with a mixture of sand and sieved **leafmould**, the important thing being that the materials are free from **weeds** and **disease** spores.

Seed saving the practice of collecting your own seed. You can harvest your own seed from many plants, both **vegetables** and **flowers**. This is one way of getting **organic seeds** and saves you money, particularly if you want large quantities for seedling crops or **sprouting**, for example. It is also necessary if you want to keep growing old **varieties** for which you can no longer buy seed.

A few simple rules for seed saving apply to all crops: feed and water the seeding plants well; allow the seeds to mature on the plant; save the seeds from the best plants and not from those that go to seed too quickly; and make sure that the seed is dry before collecting and storing it.

However, there are practical problems with some crops. Firstly, many will cross-pollinate with other varieties nearby and sometimes even with **weeds** of the same family, so that the seeds may produce hybrids – **brassicas** are notorious for this. Secondly, seeds may take a long time to mature, making it difficult to collect viable seed outdoors, particularly in cold, wet regions. Some **diseases** are also transmitted by seeds, but this is not a common problem.

Seeds, organic see **Organic seeds**.

Seed sowing the scattering or placing of seeds, either outside in a seedbed or under cover in a **greenhouse** or on a windowsill. It is important that the seeds have the right conditions to germinate and grow quickly, since both seeds and young seedlings are very vulnerable to **pest** and **disease** attack. In general, seeds do better at high temperatures, although not if it is too hot. Similarly, they need to be moist, although too much moisture will cool them down and drive out air, which is also essential.

It is easier to strike the correct balance in a greenhouse. Here you can sow seeds in pots, then prick them out into trays to grow on, before transplanting them. Alternatively, sow them in individual pots or modular trays. This system is best for plants which do not like to be transplanted. Always use a good organic "multipurpose" or **seed compost**.

If sowing outside, it is essential that the top 3 to 5 cm (1 to 2in) of the seedbed has a good **soil structure**. A **mulch** of **leafmould** or **compost** is a good long term way of ensuring this, although **digging** the bed and leaving it exposed to the **frost** is the best short-term solution on heavy **soils**. Before sowing, rake the bed to give a fine tilth, so that the seeds will have good contact with the soil. Whether sowing in drills or broadcasting, do not sow too thickly since over-crowding can encourage disease.

Guidelines on **sowing times** and depths are usually given on seed packets. In general, sow deeper in lighter soils than in heavier ones.

Seed storage the practice of storing harvested seed for use in future years. It is important to store seeds properly if they are to last from one year to the next, otherwise they will lose their vigour and ability to germinate. Keep them dry and at a low temperature: in such conditions, they can keep for several years. The actual storage life depends on the crop. With **tomatoes**, for example, it can be up to ten years, whereas for leeks it is only about three, and for parsnips only one.

Seed storage
Sewage sludge
Shallots
Shasta daisy
Shredders

Sewage sludge treated human **waste** as supplied by some waste treatment plants as a **natural fertilizer**. Although in theory an excellent form of **recycling**, in practice, most treated sewage contains industrial effluents, including heavy metals, and thus is not suitable for use in **organic gardening**. Of the various attempts to bypass this problem, including the use of **compost toilets**, no really satisfactory method has yet been developed.

Shallots see **Onions**.

Shasta daisy a hardy perennial, *Chrysanthemum maximum*, of which **varieties** with single flowerheads are good **attractant plants**. They have large, white, daisy-like flowers, and will grow on any well-drained, sunny site.

Shredders machines for chopping up tough plant material for use on a **compost heap** or as a **mulch**. There are both electric- and petrol-driven models and you can sometimes get second-hand, manual shredders.

The size of the machine you require will depend on the thickness of the material that you want to shred and how much there is of it. Larger machines will shred thicker materials, and process a large volume of material more quickly. The most powerful shredders are petrol driven, but there are electric models which are adequate for most gardens and less noisy.

154

Shrubs perennial, woody plants that form a framework to the garden as well as providing food and shelter for wildlife. They also produce a shady **habitat** for different types of plant and insect. Try to include some native shrubs in any scheme, since these attract most wildlife. However, many non-native species are good additional sources of nectar, pollen, seeds, and berries.

   Birds are attracted by the berries of shrubs, such as **pyracantha**, while all evergreens will give them good shelter in winter. **Bees** and **butterflies** have particular favourites, such as **cotoneaster** and **buddleia**. Those that flower in early spring, for example, certain mahonias and viburnums, provide nectar for insects awakening from hibernation.

Silty soil a **soil type** with some characteristics in common with **clay**. Silty soils tend to be heavy and cold when wet, and dry into hard clods. They are, however, often very fertile and benefit if you add **organic matter**.

Silver leaf a serious fungal **disease** of **plums**, which also affects some other woody plants, including **apples**, **cherries**, **gooseberries**, **currants**, **hawthorn**, and roses. Leaves become silvery, usually on one branch initially, and the disease then spreads, although not necessarily to the whole tree. Affected branches have a dark brown discolouration in the wood and often die back. Bracket-shaped **fungi** develop from the dead branches in late summer, producing spores which spread the infection through wounds in the wood during the winter.

   Avoid **pruning** susceptible trees from October to March when infection is likely. *Trichoderma viride*, which was previously used as a **biological control** for silver leaf, is no longer available in the UK.

   Silvering of leaves may also occur as a result of drought or **mineral deficiency**. To be sure that the cause is silver leaf, wait for staining and death of branches, then prune out infected parts of the tree.

Simazine a soil-acting **herbicide** used alone or in mixtures as a general weedkiller or for total **weed control** on areas where there are no food crops. Many data gaps exist for this **pesticide**, but it is a mild poison and an eye and skin **irritant**. In the USSR, cases of acute **dermatitis** have been reported after use of this chemical. Evidence exists that it is an animal **mutagen** and **oncogenic**. It reduces **earthworm** numbers for three to four months after planting, and is very **persistent** in the **soil**. Some species of **weed** show resistance to this chemical. Do all you can to avoid harming earthworms and try hand **weeding**, **hoeing**, or apply a **mulch** to clear vegetation from large areas of ground.

Slowworm a legless lizard with a uniformly greyish brown back. It is snakelike in form but completely harmless. Slowworms are good **natural predators** and will eat **slugs** and **snails**. They will live happily in your garden if there is enough long vegetation and some rocks, wood, or similar material for them to hide beneath.

Slowworm
Slug

Slug a mollusc with a vestigial or very small shell, often not visible to the naked eye. Slugs are hermaphrodite and many have elaborate courtship rituals. They are perhaps the most persistent and damaging of all garden **pests**, capable of destroying whole **vegetable** beds in just a few nights. Conventionally, slug killers, or **molluscicides**, usually in the form of slug pellets are used to counter slugs, but these can have severe environmental side effects, causing the deaths of a range of pets and garden wildlife, including **birds**, **hedgehogs**, **frogs**, and **toads** – all **natural predators** of slugs. They are also poisonous to humans, and children are particularly vulnerable.

There are a number of safer alternatives approved of by organic gardeners, of which the most effective is probably encouraging a healthy population of natural predators, such as hedgehogs and toads. Other options include: partially burying a dish of beer, or beer **trap**, in the **soil** to attract slugs (be sure to raise the lip of the dish slightly above ground level to prevent **ground beetles** falling in); erecting a **barrier** of jagged **egg shell** pieces to prevent slugs from reaching plants (an effective method under cover but easily rendered useless by rain); using a pitfall trap (see **Ground beetle**); covering individual plants with **bottle cloches**; or collecting the slugs yourself.

Collecting them by hand is surprisingly effective if continued over several consecutive nights, ideally in wet weather when the slugs will be feeding. However, incoming slugs will replace those you remove, so you will need to repeat **handpicking** periodically throughout the time your plants are at risk. The most humane way to kill slugs is by squashing them, but if you cannot face doing this, alternatives include dropping them in salty water. You can also collect slugs by day if you leave obvious objects, such as tiles or large flat stones, for them to shelter under in your planting beds. Decoys are another possible control method. Some gardeners, for example, find that slugs prefer wilted **comfrey** leaves to most crops and that a barrier of this plant will distract them from attacking seedlings. Each control method has its champions and detractors, and you will need to experiment in order to find the one that works best for you.

Slug killers see **Molluscicides**.

Snail a shelled mollusc, closely related to **slugs** and presenting the organic gardener with similar problems. Snails are slightly less of a problem to deal with in that they do not tend to burrow underground, and are thus easier to find under stones or in other sheltered spaces. The song thrush is one of the few **birds** to eat snails; it usually breaks the shells on one particular stone in its territory, which is known as the "thrush's anvil". Any of the control methods recommended under **Slugs** may also be effective in dealing with snails.

Snake a reptile, which is a rare garden visitor. Britain has only two species which are at all common: the adder, or viper, which is poisonous and lives on heaths and moors, and the non-poisonous grass snake, which can grow much larger and was previously widely distributed in lowland areas, but is now declining. These species need conserving, so take care not to harm any you find in your garden. In reciprocation, they will eat **mice**, but, unfortunately, also **frogs** and **toads**.

Soapy water see **Insecticidal soap**.

Sodium chlorate a **translocated** and soil-acting **herbicide**, used alone or in mixtures with **atrazine** and **2,4-D**, for total **weed control** in areas where there are no food crops. It is a poison and an eye and skin **irritant**, and has been identified as a potential **mutagen**. It has a long **persistence** and you should avoid using it near garden plants you want to keep, since their roots can take up lethal doses. Some formulations can render material, such as plant debris, paper, clothing, and timber, highly flammable if contaminated and allowed to dry. Sodium chlorate can do long-term damage to garden **soil** and plants. Try hand **weeding**, **hoeing**, or apply a **mulch** instead.

Sodium monochloracetate a **contact herbicide** used against a wide range of **weeds** around **brassica** seedlings, **leeks**, and **onions**. It is highly poisonous and an **irritant**, causing rashes and, sometimes, eruptions to occur on skin contact. It is harmful to pets, wild animals, and to **bees**, and may damage plants if used in warm conditions or before **frost**. Try hand **weeding**, **hoeing**, or apply a **mulch** instead.

Sodium tetraborate see **Borax**.

Soft soap a liquid soap, available from ironmongers and used as a wetting agent in the garden. Soft soap also works against **aphids** but it is not an approved **insecticide**.

Soil the top layer of earth in the garden consisting of rock particles (often ranging in size from pebbles and sand to microscopic pieces of silt or clay) mixed up with **organic matter**, water, air, various naturally occurring chemicals and elements, **microorganisms**, and larger creatures such as **earthworms**. Maintaining the health of the soil is vital to successful **organic gardening**. To do this, you need to know the **soil type** in your garden and its **nutrient** content, both of which you can discover through **soil testing**.

   Once you know what type of soil you are dealing with and have taken the necessary measures to correct any nutrient or **mineral deficiencies**, you should keep to the guidelines given below in order to ensure a good **soil structure** and continued **soil fertility**.

   Create a good **humus** content through regular application of **compost**, **mulches**, and other **biodegradable** materials. Encourage a healthy soil life by avoiding use of any toxic materials, such as **pesticides**, which can harm **earthworms** and soil microlife. Prevent depletion of plant nutrients and a build up of soil **pests** through a well-planned **rotation**. Avoid damaging the soil structure through **compaction** or over-**cultivation**. Lastly, keep alert to any warning signs of imbalances in soil quality or deficiencies and take appropriate steps to correct them.

Sodium
monochlor-
acetate

Sodium
tetraborate

Soft soap

Soil

Soil deficiencies lack of elements in the soil that are vital to healthy plant growth. Deficient **soils** include: those that are lacking in essential **minerals**, **nutrients**, or **trace elements**; those that have an **acid** or **alkaline** imbalance; and those that have insufficient **humus** and therefore a poor **soil structure**. You can detect soil deficiencies by the presence of **indicator species**, plants which only thrive in certain conditions. Alternatively, buy a simple **soil-testing** kit, which may only test for **pH**, or pay for a professional analysis.

Soil erosion see **Erosion**.

Soil fertility a measure of the **soil**'s richness in terms of **nutrients**, **humus**, and other soil matter. A fertile soil should contain all nutrients needed for plant growth in forms accessible to plant roots. A good **soil structure**, a suitable **pH**, and a flourishing population of **microorganisms** are also essential. The best way to improve the fertility of most soils is to add **organic matter**.

Soil structure the physical structure of the **soil**, and one of the most important factors affecting **soil fertility**. A soil with a good structure contains a network of spaces which allow aeration and **drainage**, while retaining good reserves of moisture. The spaces are formed when soil particles combine to form larger "crumbs" of varying sizes, which you can see if you crush a small clod of soil in your hand.

Whether you have a **sandy** or **clay soil**, the way to improve the structure is to add **organic matter**. This helps to bind together fine soil particles and to break up large clods of soil, giving a good crumb structure. It is also important not to damage the structure by, for example, treading on the soil (see **Compaction**) or cultivating it when it is wet.

Soil temperature the internal temperature of the soil. If soil becomes too cold, especially in times of **frost**, plants will not grow properly, and seeds will be unable to **germinate**. The germination temperatures of different plants vary widely, so it is worthwhile checking up on these in seed catalogues or books before **sowing** outdoors, particularly in early spring. You can also buy a soil thermometer.

Mulches are a good way of keeping the soil warm, particularly in winter when there is little, or no, plant cover. However, you need to choose your materials carefully. ▷

Light-coloured materials, such as **newspaper** and gravel, for example, will keep the soil cold, whereas clear **polythene** will warm it up. Mulches of organic material generally have an insulating effect, tending to keep the temperature the same as when the mulch was applied.

Soil testing the practice, essential in any garden, of establishing the **soil type**, its **pH**, and its **nutrient** content. To test for pH, either send a soil sample away for analysis or use a do-it-yourself soil-testing kit. If your plants exhibit signs of **mineral deficiencies** at normal pH levels, or if you are starting work in a new garden, then it is also wise to test the soil nutrient content. Although there are do-it-yourself kits for this, it is more reliable to send a sample for analysis, particularly if you can find a service specifically for organic growers (see Useful Addresses, pp. 190-1). See **Soil types** for information on how to test for soil type.

Soil types the principle types of **soil: clay**, **sand**, and **silt**. In general, the size of the **mineral** particles in the soil determines its type. Sand has the largest particles and clay the smallest. Loams are a mixture of sand, silt, and clay, but they are described by the type predominating. It is important to find out what type of soil you have, since this will determine how easy it is to work, how well it drains, and to what extent it holds **nutrients**. In turn, such factors will indicate how you should manage it and what plants you should grow. Rubbing the soil between your fingers will give you some indication of type: a clay soil feels sticky, a silty soil has a silky texture, and a sandy soil is gritty.

Solar greenhouse a type of **greenhouse** design which saves on **energy** costs by using **solar heating** to extend the growing season. **Solar panels** enhance its effectiveness.

Solar heating, passive a low-cost form of heating, both in terms of installation and use, which relies on sound design techniques to maximize the amount of solar radiation that enters, and stays inside, a building, thus reducing the amount of **energy** needed for heating. Many passive solar buildings rely entirely on orientation, number and position of windows, and use of **insulation**, including blinds which either absorb or reflect the sun's heat, depending on temperature needs. In a passive-**solar greenhouse**, the outer walls may be made of double- or triple-glazed glass or **plastic** for maximum absorption of heat. These may be complimented by insulating devices, such as thick internal masonry walls and water-filled drums. Roof and floor vents release excess heat and allow cool air to enter.

Solar panels glass- or plastic-covered collector panels, which are fixed to sun-facing roofs as a method of collecting solar energy for home use. There are two basic types: those that collect the heat energy from the sun and use it for heating water or air, which passes through or around the panelling in pipes or ducts; and those that contain solar electric cells, which convert light energy from the sun directly into electricity.

Soot a material commonly added to the **compost heap**. However, soot contains **carcinogens** and is not recommended for use in **organic gardening**.

Sowing see **Seed sowing**.

Sowing times recommended times for **seed sowing**. By adjusting sowing times, you can avoid the worst periods of attack by some **pests**. For example, **peas** sown early or very late will suffer less damage by **pea moth** maggots, while very early or late sowings of **brassicas** will miss the worst **fleabeetle** attacks. However, it is never worth sowing any crop outside too early before the **soil** has warmed up, since slowly germinating seedlings are more vulnerable to pests and **diseases**. Wait for a few weeks, or use a sheet of clear **plastic** or **cloches** to warm up the soil.

Spider a generally harmless arthropod invertebrate, which is a **natural predator** of flies, flying **aphids**, and other **pests**.

Spinach an annual **vegetable**, cultivated for its green leaves. The leaves of true spinach, *Spinacea oleracea*, are said to have the best "spinachy" flavour. However, true spinach runs to seed quickly, especially in the heat, so you will need to make successive sowings. Summer crops of it are best grown in light shade. In hot, dry conditions, the half-hardy New Zealand spinach, *Tetragonia expansa*, is more likely to succeed. Spinach beet, *Beta vulgaris*, is easier to grow since it will last a whole season. Swiss chard, with

161

thick white stems, and the red-stemmed ruby chard, are closely related to spinach beet and you should grow them in the same way. These types of spinach and chard need a **soil** rich in **organic matter** and plenty of moisture. Grow them with beetroot in your crop **rotation**. They are all relatively trouble free: **slugs** and **birds** may attack young leaves and downy **mildew** can be a problem – look out for **resistant varieties**, where available.

Spot treatment the use of a special applicator to apply **herbicides** to individual **weed** species in beds, on **lawns**, on **paths**, or on patios. This is a far less hazardous method of application than spraying, and time-consuming since you have to go round again to pick up the dead plants. Hand **weeding** is quicker, cheaper, and above all hazard free.

Spray a hand-held sprayer, commonly used to apply garden **pesticides**. This method of application is potentially hazardous because very small droplets are liable to create **spray drift** whatever the weather conditions. There is also a high risk of personal contamination, either through getting caught in spray drift or as a result of liquid dribbling down from the nozzle. Even if you are applying the safest of pesticides, such as **insecticidal soap**, you should still wear gloves and clothes which cover your arms and legs. If you get any of the spray on your skin, wash it off promptly with plenty of water. If any reaches your eyes, rinse them out well and consult a doctor.

Spray drift the accidental drift of a **pesticide spray** away from the target area. Spray drift can unintentionally kill garden plants and wildlife, contaminate **fruit** and **vegetables** with pesticide **residues**, and generally endanger human health, although its effects are not always immediately obvious. Even if spraying is done in calm conditions, some contamination is almost inevitable due to the variable nature of the **spray** droplets, the smallest of which tend to drift in any conditions. Some pesticides are also volatile.

If you are the victim of a spray drift incident, and your vegetables are contaminated, find out which chemical has been used and its **harvest interval**. You can claim damages for injury to your own health or to your garden, but if you have to go through the courts, this can be a lengthy and expensive process with no certain outcome.

Sprinkler an **irrigation** system designed to water plants by spraying small droplets over them; there are various types that work in different ways. Sprinklers are useful for **watering** seedbeds and intensely planted **vegetable** beds. Choose one with a fine **spray**, because large droplets hitting the soil with force can damage the **soil structure**.

Sprinklers have three main problems. Firstly, watering from overhead can spoil **fruit** and **flowers**, and encourage fungal disease. Secondly, it is difficult not to waste water on **paths** or adjacent crops. Lastly, water tends to be lost by evaporation from the surface. In some cases, **trickle systems** are a better and less wasteful alternative.

Sprouting the practice of germinating seeds indoors and allowing them to grow for only a few days before you harvest them. You can use sprouts in salads and a variety of other dishes. Many seeds are suitable for sprouting, for example, those of mung beans and other **legumes**, **brassicas**, such as cabbage, and cereals, for example, wheat.

Sprout seeds in any container, keeping them warm and moist, and rinse them regularly. Eat them lightly cooked or raw (when they are at their most nutritious), although some legume seeds can be harmful if eaten raw in large quantities. By sprouting seeds you can produce fresh, nutritious food, even without a garden, but make sure the seed that you buy has not been treated with chemicals. Alternatively, do your own **seed saving**.

Squashes plants whose edible fruit come in all shapes and sizes. Summer squashes include marrows and courgettes, and any other squashes that you can eat fresh from the plant. Winter squashes include pumpkins and squashes that develop tough skins for storage. All squashes are members of the **cucumber** family (Cucurbitaceae). They will not tolerate **frost**, and need a fairly sunny, sheltered site and a **soil** rich in **organic matter**. Choose bush varieties if space is limited, or allow trailing varieties to run through tall crops, such as **sweetcorn**. Squashes are relatively trouble free, although **slugs** and **aphids** may damage young plants. The main diseases are powdery **mildew** and **cucumber mosaic virus**, but look out for **resistant varieties**.

Squirrel an agile mammal that occasionally visits gardens. It feeds on nuts and seeds and makes nests, called drays, in tall trees. In the UK, there are two species: the native red squirrel and the introduced grey squirrel. The latter has almost completely displaced the red squirrel, which is now confined to specific areas in the British Isles.

Squirrels may attack nestlings and eat eggs and they will occasionally take over **nest boxes** if they can get inside. The grey squirrel is a **pest** in woodland because of its bark-stripping activities. But unless you are growing young trees, you should welcome these animals in your garden.

Stable manure horse droppings which are a useful source of **manure** for the gardener. If you have a horse stable nearby, you can collect it for free, or arrange for it to be delivered for a small charge. It is always best to compost manure before use (see under **Manure**).

Storage, vegetable various methods of storing harvested **vegetables**. **Onions, potatoes**, and winter **squashes** all store well in the right conditions. Put potatoes and squashes in strong, paper or hessian sacks in a dry, **frost**-free place. Onions are better at lower temperatures, ideally 32°F (0°C), but must have good ventilation, so hanging them in nets or stringing them on ropes works well.

Many **root crops** keep best if left in the ground. However, if you need to lift them because of possible **pest** damage or severe frosts, store them in cool, moist conditions, for example, in boxes of sand or in **polythene** bags containing some ventilation holes.

Straw a fairly long-lasting **mulch**, and one that will add **organic matter** and a few plant **nutrients** to the **soil** if allowed to decay. It is also a good material for protecting **root crops** against **frost**, and for adding to a **compost heap**, which contains too many sappy materials. Do not dig it into the soil, however, since it can cause depletion of **nitrogen**. Bought-in straw is likely to contain **herbicide residues** so you should leave it to weather for at least six months before use. This will give residues a chance to decompose.

Strawberry a low-growing plant, which you will have space for even in the smallest garden. If you have no room in the beds, you can plant strawberries in pots or tubs, or even in hanging baskets. The bushy alpine varieties are ideal for edging a **flower**bed, and are good **attractant plants**.

164

A few strawberry plants in the **greenhouse** will give you an early crop, while "perpetual fruiting" varieties can extend the season into the autumn. Strawberries like a sunny site and a well-drained **soil** with plenty of **organic matter**. To avoid the build up of **disease**, you need to replace plants about every three years and move them to a different spot. It is therefore often convenient to fit them into your vegetable **rotation**. The main strawberry **pests** are **birds, slugs, aphids**, and **red spider mites. Botrytis, mildew**, and **virus diseases** are also a problem. Always buy virus-free stock, and look out for **resistant varieties**.

Sulphur an important micro-**nutrient** in the **soil**. At the moment, sulphur is seldom in short supply because of deposition of the air pollutant, sulphur dioxide. However, you can use **gypsum** to raise levels, if necessary.

Swedes see **Brassicas**.

Sweetcorn a tall **vegetable**, cultivated for its edible kernel, which is best eaten straight from the garden, although new "supersweet" varieties keep their sweetness for longer after picking. Sweetcorn needs a fertile **soil** and a hot, sunny position. In cool climates, use quickly maturing **varieties**. Sweetcorn is not closely related to any other vegetables, and so will fit anywhere in a crop **rotation**. Plant it in blocks rather than rows to help ensure **pollination** by the wind. You can try **intercropping** it with short or trailing crops. **Slugs** attack the young plants, but otherwise sweetcorn is relatively trouble free.

Symbiosis a mutually beneficial relationship between different plant or animal species, for example, the association that exists between **nitrogen**-fixing **bacteria** and **legumes**, such as **peas** and **beans**.

Systemic pesticide a type of **pesticide** that enters the body of a plant and is taken up by a **pest** or **disease** pathogen before destroying it. **Persistent** systemic pesticides leave **residues** in plants, which cannot simply be washed away, and may later poison organisms that feed on the plant, including **beneficial insects** and **fungi**.

2,4,5-T a **translocated herbicide**, used to control woody **weeds** and **nettles**. 2,4,5-T is notorious for being one of the constituents of Agent Orange, a defoliant used to destroy huge areas of vegetation during the Vietnam war. In the past, certain makes of 2,4,5-T were heavily contaminated with dioxins, some of which were potent **carcinogens** and **teratogens**. Although the dioxin levels in 2,4,5-T today are supposed to be far lower, there is evidence that the **pesticide** itself is a carcinogen, teratogen, and **mutagen**. 2,4,5-T is also a poison and an **irritant**. It is dangerous to fish and can cause damage through **spray drift**. It has been banned, withdrawn, or severely restricted in at least 15 countries. In Britain, 2,4,5-T has been voluntarily withdrawn by many local authorities and other major users, but is still sold in many garden centres. Instead of destroying nettles, collect them to make a **liquid feed** or add them directly to the **compost heap** since they are rich in **nitrogen**. Alternatively, try forking or using a **mulch**.

Tagetes minuta a plant that has the reputation of keeping the invasive roots of **weeds** at bay, such as couch grass and ground elder. It is a tall relation of the French **marigold** and similarly half hardy. This gives it little time to be effective in cool climates.

Tares an annual **green manure**, *Vicia sativa*, which you can sow in spring to cover ground for two to three months, or

166

in late summer to overwinter. It is a **legume** which fixes **nitrogen** and is good for suppressing **weeds**. Dig it in at any time before it flowers (see **Green manures** chart, pp. 80-1).

Tar oil an **insecticide** and defoliant spray used against over-wintering insect **pests** and their larvae; it is also used to counter powdery **mildew** and to prevent the spread of **moss** and **lichen**. It is strongly poisonous, an eye, skin, and res-piratory system **irritant**, and can also cause **dermatitis** in the presence of sunlight. Tar oil can kill **beneficial insects** and is dangerous to pets, wildlife, and fish. Try **cultural control**, **biological control**, **traps**, and **barriers** instead. Only resort to the use of **natural insecticides**, such as **derris** and **insecticidal soap**, if all else fails.

Tecanzene a **fungicide** and growth regulator, used alone or with **gamma HCH** against dry **rot** and **botrytis**. It is an eye, skin, and respiratory system **irritant** and there is some evi-dence that it is **oncogenic**. It is harmful to fish and has a long **persistence**, with **harvest intervals** of two to six weeks. Tecanzene is one of the **pesticides** that has surpassed the **Maximum Residue Level** in Britain. Try **cultural control** instead.

Teratogen any substance or process that can cause or con-tribute to birth defects. For the problems of identifying teratogens, see **Carcinogen**.

Tetramethrin a **contact insecticide** of the **pyrethroid** group, often used in mixtures. There is some evidence that it is a **carcinogen**. It is dangerous to fish and toxic to **bees**. Try **cul-tural control**, **biological control**, **traps**, and **barriers** instead. Only use **natural insecticides**, such as **derris**, if all else fails.

Thiophanate methyl a **systemic fungicide** used on **vegetables**, grains, and turf, with similar properties to **benomyl**. It is an eye, skin, and respiratory system **irritant**. Finland and the USA have restricted use of this pesticide because of the carcinogenic and mutagenic risks posed by one of its breakdown products. It is weakly toxic to fish and has moderate **persistence**. At least 13 pathogens show **resistance** to thiophanate methyl. Try **cultural control** instead.

Thiram a **fungicide** with a wide variety of uses, including treatment of seeds. It is a poison (producing toxic gases

Tar oil
Tecanzene
Teratogen
Tetramethrin
Thiophanate
methyl
Thiram

when burnt), an eye, skin, and respiratory system **irritant**, and a suspected **mutagen** and **teratogen**. Thiram is moderately **persistent**. Use untreated seeds, and **cultural control** for preventing fungal **disease**.

Thrips tiny, cylindrical insects, many of which are **pests** of garden and **greenhouse** plants. They commonly affect **onions**, **peas**, and broad **beans**, and the flowers of ornamentals, such as gladioli and roses, causing mottling or silvering and some distortion. Attacks are worse in hot, dry conditions. To help prevent this pest, water regularly and, in greenhouses, maintain a cool, humid atmosphere. Winter **digging** of infested plots and greenhouse **hygiene** will reduce the number of pests overwintering. As a last resort only, try spraying with **insecticidal soap**.

Timber, sustainable any timber that comes from a sustainably managed system, which can either indicate selective felling from a natural forest or a well-managed plantation. Widespread loss of tree cover, or deforestation, poses one of the major environmental threats of our time, so it is important to use timber with care in the garden. Avoid **tropical hardwoods** and, where possible, reuse wood for making **compost bins**, **fencing**, and garden sheds. Failing that, it is probably best to use British-grown hardwoods or European softwoods. The dark, inner heartwood of British-grown oaks, sweet chesnuts, larches, Douglas firs, and cedars is resistant to rotting but all other native species will quickly succumb once in contact with the **soil**, unless chemically pretreated. European softwoods are relatively quick growers and therefore more likely to be subjects for plantation management, although in practice it is often difficult to obtain firm guarantees from suppliers that the wood they sell is from a sustainable source. See **Timber treatment** for advice on environmentally acceptable methods of treating wood. See also **Recycling**.

Timber treatment any treatment for increasing the resistance of **timber** to insect, bacterial, and fungal attack and the damaging effects of sunlight and frost. Although a lot of research still remains to be done on the safety of various timber treatments, the following are some of the less hazardous: boron and its salts (which include **borax**), and various wood pitch preservatives, which work by repelling water so that timber is too dry for bacterial action to start. (Borax and **permethrin** are both recommended as relatively safe for use on roofing timber where **bats** are likely to roost.) Professionally "tanalised" timber is probably less harmful than most **wood preservative** treatments, since the chemicals used are locked closely into the wood and **leaching** is less likely to occur. Nevertheless, you should always wear gloves when handling tanalised timber. Alternatively, you can opt for untreated timber, and just accept that it will not last so long, or use more durable timber (see **Timber, sustainable**). Always make **nest boxes** and bat and **bird** boxes out of untreated timber.

Toad an amphibious, harmless creature with a voracious appetite for **slugs** and other **pests**. They usually only remain in a garden if there are areas of thick vegetation that are likely to remain damp, and, to breed, they need water. Building up a colony is a good long-term solution to inevitable slug problems, but getting adult toads to adopt a garden other than by choice is difficult because they invariably return to their original home to breed. Only occasionally will they adopt a pond spontaneously for the purpose. You can introduce toad spawn from outside, but you must ask permission from your local Wildlife Trust (see Useful Addresses, pp. 190-91). Avoid use of slug pellets since these are lethal to toads, as are slugs that have been poisoned by them.

Tomatoes a vitamin-rich **vegetable** and salad crop. Tomatoes are half hardy and, in a cool climate, you need to grow them in a sunny, sheltered position or in a **greenhouse** in order to get a good crop of ripe fruit. Upright varieties need staking and training, but can give high yields, especially indoors, and the fruit is out of reach of any **slugs**. Bush varieties need less attention. They are useful for growing outdoors under **cloches**, and you can plant dwarf types in pots, or even in hanging baskets. Tomatoes need a fertile, well-drained **soil**.

The plants are susceptible to several soil-borne **diseases**, so move them from year to year, even in a greenhouse. Alternatively, replace the soil in the greenhouse with fresh soil. Outside, grow tomatoes with **potatoes** in your crop **rotation**. Those grown in pots or **growbags** will need regular **watering** with a **liquid feed** once fruit begins to form. ▷

Tomatoes also suffer from **blossom end rot** and **potato and tomato blight**, while in the greenhouse, **whitefly** is usually the main **pest**. Look out for the modern greenhouse varieties, which have resistance to some soil-borne diseases.

Tools, garden any implement designed to facilitate garden tasks. From an environmental perspective, the best tools are those that are well made, long lasting, and do not require any energy to work. Regularly clean, dry, and oil metal parts and keep the tools stored under cover.

Tortrix moths a group of small moths, whose green **caterpillars** are **pests** of **apples**, **pears**, **plums**, and **cherries**. They feed on buds, leaves, and fruit, spinning silken threads which draw the leaves together around them to form a protective cover. Damage is not usually serious. Use **handpicking** to remove any caterpillars that you find.

Trace elements mineral elements, such as iron and zinc, that are needed only in small amounts by plants, but which are essential for healthy growth. Bleaching between the veins of young leaves may be a sign of iron deficiency.

Translocated herbicide a type of **herbicide**, which is taken into a **weed** at a particular point. From there it travels around the rest of the plant, damaging and eventually killing the whole organism.

Trap any device that is used to catch **pests**. Easy-to-make traps include: beer traps for **slugs**, **grease bands** for **winter moths**, and sticky boards for catching **fleabeetles** as they jump. There are also traps for **codling moths** which use a synthetic sex attractant (pheromone) to lure in the males. Traps can be effective in reducing pest numbers if you use them regularly, although on their own they are unlikely to be a long-term method of control. See **Ground beetle** for details on the pitfall trap.

Tree a major role player in the garden **ecology**, protecting the **soil** and plants growing beneath it from excesses of sun, wind, and rain, and providing shelter for wildlife.
  You can grow trees either from seeds or in some cases, as with **willow**, from **cuttings**. Some seeds need special treatment, for example, burying, soaking, or splitting –

consult a specialist book for advice. Specialist seed dealers
sell tree seeds, but it is cheaper to collect your own seeds
in the autumn from locally grown trees.

Include species native to Britain since these will attract
the most wildlife: **ash** and **oak** are suitable for larger
gardens, while for smaller plots, trees such as the silver
birch are ideal. You can also incorporate native trees into
a **hedge**. Plant traditional varieties of **apples**, **pears**, and
other **fruit** for food. Some non-native trees, such as the
ornamental **crab apple**, are also good for wildlife.

Trefoil a **green manure**, *Medicago lupulina*. Grow it as an
annual or biennial to cover ground for up to a year. It is a
legume and will fix **nitrogen**. Dig it in at any time when it is
fresh and green (see **Green manures** chart, pp. 80-1).

Trench composting an alternative to the **compost heap**, useful
for dealing with **household scraps** and the small amounts of
garden debris available in winter, including **brassica** stems.
Tip these materials into a trench where you are going to
grow **peas** or runner **beans** the following year. Layer with
lime and **soil**, and leave for at least two months before sowing or planting. Peas and runner beans are **legumes** which
fix **nitrogen**, so there is no depletion of the soil as the material decays. However, this system can attract **rats**.

Trichlorfon a non-**systemic insecticide** of the **organophosphorus**
group, used against **cabbage root fly** and **caterpillars**. It is a
poison, which may be swallowed, inhaled, or absorbed
through the skin, and will release toxic fumes if heated.
Trichlorfon is an **anticholinesterase** compound, a mild skin
irritant, and evidence exists that it may be a **mutagen** and **teratogen**. There is a **harvest interval** of at least two days. It is
harmful to fish.

Trichoderma viride a fungus that is antagonistic to a number
of harmful **fungi**, most notably those that cause **silver leaf
disease** of **plums** and other trees. It has been formulated
into both a powder and pellets, both of which are useful
forms of **biological control** against the disease, although
unfortunately neither are now available in the UK. To
treat an affected tree or to protect one at risk, pellets are
inserted into holes drilled in a spiral around the trunk,
while the powder is made into a paste for painting on to

Trefoil
Trench
composting
Trichlorfon
*Trichoderma
viride*

171

pruning cuts. *Trichoderma viride* has also been investigated as a control for **Dutch elm disease**.

Trickle systems various systems of **irrigation** that make use of different types of hose pipe, all designed to release drips of water slowly along their length. Seep hoses are flat when empty and allow water to seep out along their length through a machine seam. Trickle hoses are rigid with discrete holes, from which water trickles out. You can also get pipes which are porous along their whole length so water only seeps out when the **soil** is dry. Trickle or seep hoses are ideal for delivering water to plant roots without wastage, particularly if you run them along the ground under a **mulch**. They have several advantages over **sprinklers** in that they do no damage to **fruit** or **flowers**, are less likely to cause fungal **diseases**, and use less water.

Tropical hardwood any timber obtained from tropical hardwood trees. Avoid purchasing tropical hardwoods for use in the garden since their continued existence is under threat due to widespread deforestation carried out in tropical areas. They are unlikely to come from sustainably managed sources. See **Timber, sustainable** for advice on alternative types of wood to use.

Tumbler a barrel-shaped container for making **compost**, mounted so that you can rotate it. Fill the barrel with the same materials that you would use in a **compost heap**, then turn it several times each day. This will keep **aerobic bacterial decomposition** going and, as long as the tumbler is large enough to carry sufficient material, the contents heat up well. After only a few weeks, it will produce a rough compost which you can use directly or stack under cover.

Turnips see **Brassicas**.

Umbellifers plants belonging to the family Umbelliferae, usually characterised by flat umbrella-like flowerheads, or umbels. Many **herbs** belong to this family, for example, fennel, dill, and angelica, and so do some common **weeds**. Several **vegetables**, such as **carrots**, **parsnips**, and **celery**, are also umbellifers, although as they are biennial you do not usually see their flowers, unless they bolt or you leave them to seed. Most umbellifers are good **attractant plants** for **beneficial insects**, such as **hoverflies**.

Urine a **nitrogen**-rich **compost activator**. If added to a **compost heap** composed mainly of fibrous plant material, urine will help to ensure the correct **carbon-nitrogen ratio**.

Variety a cultivated strain of a plant. There are some varieties of **fruit**, **vegetables**, and **flowers** that are particularly suitable for organic growers. Those that show **resistance** to particular **pests** and **diseases** are an obvious choice (see **Resistant varieties**). Quick-maturing vegetable varieties can also be useful. Such varieties of **potato**, for example, will have already formed a good crop of tubers before **potato blight** strikes and harvest is necessary. Similarly, fast-growing varieties of **carrot** enable late **sowing times** to avoid **carrot fly**. Varieties with floppy leaves which smother **weeds** are another possible choice. With flowers, single varieties are more likely to be better **attractant plants** than their highly bred, double counterparts. ▷

173

New varieties of vegetable and fruit are often bred with commercial growers in mind, and are not always best for gardeners. You may find that some old varieties are better tasting and have other useful qualities. Keeping them in cultivation contributes to **genetic conservation** and helps to maintain **diversity** for future plant breeders.

Vegan gardening a method of growing plants designed to exclude the use of animal products. Vegan gardening is practised by an increasing number of vegetarians and vegans and avoids the use of **pesticides** and **natural fertilizers** based on animal products, such as **manure**, **bone meal**, and **fish meal**. To substitute for **nitrogen**-rich manure, cultivate **green manures** or apply **comfrey**, **nettle liquid feed**, or domestic **urine**, as available.

Vegetables a wide-ranging group of edible plants, including leaf and **root** crops, as well as those grown for their tubers and fruits. Organically grown vegetables are reputed to taste better than conventionally grown crops, and often store better. This is possibly because they contain less water; some may also contain more vitamins.

Most vegetable crops grow best on a fertile **soil** in an open, sunny position and thus need a prime site in your garden and a generous allocation of **compost** or **manure**. However, you do not need to hide them away – a vegetable plot can be an attractive feature. You can fit annual vegetables into a crop **rotation** to help maintain **soil fertility** and prevent the build up of **pests** and **diseases**. Many vegetables are also decorative enough to grow in a **flower** border, for example, salad crops, and perennials such as globe **artichokes**.

Vine weevil a weevil, whose white larvae are a serious **pest** of pot plants in **greenhouses** and indoors; they may also attack ornamental plants outside. The weevil larvae feed on the plant roots, causing wilting. The adult weevils hide at **soil** level in crevices and debris by day, and crawl up on to plants at night to feed and lay their eggs. Inspect the roots of any flagging pot plants carefully, destroying any larvae that you find, and repotting them immediately. Maintain good **hygiene**, so that there is no cover for adult weevils. A **biological control** for vine weevil has recently been developed for use in greenhouses.

Violet root rot a common **disease** of **beetroot, carrots, parsnips, potatoes, swedes**, and **turnips**, which sometimes affects other **vegetables**, ornamentals, and **weeds**. It usually causes a purplish rot in roots or tubers. Avoid waterlogged or **acid soils** since they favour this disease. Remove and destroy all affected plants, and keep land **weed** free. Do not grow susceptible crops for four years afterward.

Virus a very simple organism, smaller than **bacteria**, which can only survive and reproduce within the cells of plants and animals. Most forms are pathogens, causing **disease** in both plants and animals.

Virus-free stock the stock of certain virus-prone plants that is available from some suppliers with a virus-free guarantee. Virus-free stock is worth looking out for, particularly in the case of **strawberries** and **bush** and **cane fruit**.

Vole a small rodent, which will sometimes inhabit gardens. They make up for occasional damage to bulbs and **root crops** by eating invertebrate **pests**.

Create a garden to heal body, mind, and spirit, using the themes outlined below.

A fountain as a central point
Closeness to water focuses the mind and encourages contemplation and a calm, serene approach to life. **Birds** love to bathe in a fountain.

Path A gravel path interspersed with low-growing **herbs**, such as chamomile and creeping thyme, makes a scented walkway. The gravel helps to suppress **weed** growth and is also an ideal **mulch** for shrubby, sun-loving species. Boulders of varying shapes create contrasts in form.

Seat in a scented arbour
Protected, secluded areas such as these are vital, particularly if

you lead a hectic lifestyle or live in a noisy urban area. Cover the arbour with twining, aromatic **climbers**, such as hops and **honeysuckle**.

Hedges Plant lavender and hyssop to create low-growing, aromatic, flowering **hedges**.

White herbs and flowers Massed planting of white flowers and foliage plants is restful to observe, encouraging spirituality and bringing peace of mind.

Single tree Plant a small tree, such as a Japanese maple or birch, as a symbol of inner strength and vitality.

Perennial herbs Include large, non-native herbs, such as elecampagne and angelica, for

their medicinal properties. Feed them with a **mulch** of **compost**.

Native plants Grow wild plants with herbal properties, such as meadowsweet and mullein, to help attract a variety of creatures into the garden.

Aromatic herbs Keep this area for small shrubby herbs, such as thyme, sage, and rosemary, with medicinal as well as culinary uses. They need a well-drained, sunny spot. Most of these are also good **bee** plants.

Bed Sow annual herbs, such as dill and coriander, in a seed bed.

Nettles A patch of these will provide you with **liquid feed** for herbs in the **greenhouse**. They also have medicinal uses and attract **beneficial insects** and **butterflies**.

Nettle barrel Fill this with nettle leaves to make a liquid feed.

Compost bins Add herb leaves and clippings as a mineral-rich addition to the **compost heap**.

Herb drier This solar-based system dries herbs quickly for winter use and ensures that they retain their full flavour.

Windbreak You can make an effective shelter belt out of shrubs with herbal properties, such as **buckthorn** and **hawthorn**.

Greenhouse This is useful for raising plants from seeds and **cuttings** and for housing tender herbs, such as lemon verbena.

Wall a vertical structure of brick or stone, which can give privacy to the garden as well as acting as a **windbreak**. Avoid solid, high walls, since wind goes up and over them instead of filtering through, and this can create damaging eddies in their lee. Solid structures can also produce stagnant conditions which encourage **disease** and **frost** pockets.

Walls are useful for supporting **climbers**, and wall-trained **fruit** and **shrubs**. **Apples**, **pears**, **redcurrants**, and **white currants** all train well as fans, cordons, or espaliers, while **peaches**, **cherries**, and **plums** are best as fans. Training them makes good use of space, while the wall provides extra warmth and shelter for the plants. Low, retaining walls within the garden give you an ideal opportunity to grow trailing plants, either along the top or through gaps. A dry-stone wall is the best for wildlife, providing numerous nooks and crannies for insects and small mammals.

Warfarin an older type of **rodenticide** which kills **mice** and **rats** by dehydration. It is a poison, and needs to be kept well away from children and any pets. It is, however, less poisonous than some newer rodenticides. Widespread **resistance** to warfarin has developed, especially in rats, and many pest-control firms have now abandoned it. See **Rats** for safer, alternative methods of control.

Wasp a large group of flying insects, including many **parasitic wasps**. The common wasp has a smart yellow and black striped body and can sting if angry or sleepy; it is useful as a **natural predator**, rearing its offspring on insects, including many flying **pests**.

Waste any left-over product of human activity which appears to serve no immediate purpose. Modern society is the most wasteful in history, consuming vast quantities of **energy** and raw materials, an increasingly large proportion of which is employed in non-reusable goods. You can help reverse the trend, by adding **biodegradable** waste, such as **household scraps** and plant debris, to the **compost heap**, by reusing household products, by repairing garden **tools**, and by **recycling** materials wherever possible. See also **Recycling** and **Water conservation**.

Water butt a wooden or plastic barrel used to collect and store rainwater. It is usually placed under the eaves of a roof and is a valuable method of **water conservation**.

Water conservation the practice of conserving water through rainwater harvesting, reuse of household water, and economical **irrigation** techniques. If you live in an area which experiences regular droughts, water conservation will need to be a central feature of your garden design. Shade, particularly in the form of layered planting, is important in minimizing water loss and you should choose plants for their ability to withstand drought. The way in which you water your garden is also significant. Avoid applying small amounts of water which will rapidly evaporate before penetrating the **soil** to any depth, and will stimulate plants to produce shallow roots rather than the deep roots required to draw up water from further underground. An occasional heavy soak is preferable. In some hot countries, water is applied directly below the surface, through pipes laid under beds, so that evaporation loss is minimized and roots remain well underground.

You can plan for an occasional drought by installing one or more **water butts** to collect water draining from the roof, or an underground water-storage tank. **Recycling** domestic household water is a possibility but, if you do this, avoid using soapy water on **flowers** and **vegetables** since it can damage them. It is best to water in the evening when the sun is low and water is less likely to evaporate. Applying a **mulch** is another good way of reducing water loss.

179

Watering a method of ensuring that plants have a sufficient supply of water. Unless you live in a very wet region, you will almost certainly have to water seedlings and also transplants until they become established. After this, the need for watering depends on your **soil type** and the plants you grow. Plants stressed through lack of water are more susceptible to **pest** and **disease** attack, particularly from **aphids** and powdery **mildew**, and to some disorders such as **bitterpit** in **apples**. Deprived **fruit** and **vegetable** crops will give lower yields. On the other hand, overwatering can have detrimental effects, causing over leafy growth, and increasing the risk of fungal **disease**.

You can help the **soil** retain moisture by adding **organic matter** and by applying a **mulch** around the plants when it is wet. Many crops have stages of growth during which they respond best to watering. Vegetables grown for their fruit or seeds will benefit most while flowering and while the fruit or pods are developing. Leafy crops need watering throughout their growth. Fruit trees and bushes need most water when the fruit is forming, both to help it swell and to produce new growth that will support the next year's crop. Whether you water by hand or use an **irrigation** system, watering thoroughly at less frequent intervals is more beneficial than watering little and often.

Water pollution any form of **pollution** that depletes water quality. **Nitrates** and other potentially harmful substances **leaching** from artificial **fertilizers**, **manure**, and **pesticides** are likely to be the main water pollutants released from gardens. Britain already exceeds the European Community maximum with regard to levels of these pollutants in water and although farming is the chief source of leaching, gardeners can help to reduce levels by switching to safer, non-pollutant **organic gardening** products and techniques and only applying manure in spring when there are enough growing plants to take up the **nutrients**.

Water resources available supplies of water which you can use for garden **irrigation**. These include rainwater, (which you may wish to harvest in a **water butt** or underground reservoir if you live in an area that is prone to drought), tap water, and reusable household water. You can apply fairly clean household water directly or plumb your water system so that it flows into a storage tank. However, avoid use of soapy water in large quantities, because the sodium it contains can harm plants. If you use it at all, do so only in emergencies, around **fruit** trees or on **lawns**.

Weed control any method used to control unwanted plants, or **weeds**, in the garden. This does not mean eliminating all weeds, but just preventing them from smothering or seriously hampering the growth of **fruit** and **vegetable** crops and **flowers**. In **organic gardening**, chemical **herbicides** are unacceptable because of the health and environmental hazards that they pose. Use alternatives including hand **weeding**, **hoeing**, **flameweeding** on paths, forking or **digging** to remove persistent, deep-rooted weeds, **rotavating**, and various kinds of **mulch**, including **bark**, **leafmould**, **newspaper**, and **cardboard** (see chart overleaf).

Weeding the practice of removing **weeds** by hand or with a fork, which is sometimes the best way of dealing with them. Hand weeding works well, for example, with small numbers of perennial weeds, or between closely planted crops in a **bed system**. You should begin as early as you can, before the weeds start competing with your plants and getting out of control.

Weed control
Weeding
Weedkillers
Weeds

Weedkillers see **Herbicides**.

Weeds plants that are uninvited in the garden, competing with other plants for light, water, food, and space, and looking untidy. Some weeds can also harbour **pests** and **diseases**. Weeds are usually wild plants, but they can also be cultivated species that have got out of hand. Identifying them and discovering their growth habits is the first steps toward deciding the best method of **weed control**. Annual weeds, such as groundsel, are not usually difficult to control. Perennial weeds may be tap-rooted, for example, dandelion and dock, or creep along the surface, like creeping buttercup. The worst to control are those with creeping, underground stems or roots, such as ground elder, couch grass, and bindweed (see **Weed control** chart, pp. 182-3), and those with tubers or corms, for example, the lesser celandine.

However, you may not want to get rid of every weed. Some look attractive, provide food for **beneficial insects**, and make material for the **compost heap** or **liquid feeds**.

How to control weeds

**Weed control
(chart)**

Weed	Life cycle	Growing habits
Annual meadow grass *Poa annua*	Annual	Tufty; seeds almost all year round
Common chickweed *Stellaria media*	Annual	Prolific spreader on fertile **soil**; seeds almost all year round
Couch grass *Igropyron repens*	Perennial	A low-growing grass with shallow, creeping, underground stems, fragments of which will regrow
Creeping buttercup *Ranunculus repens*	Perennial	Low rosettes of leaves; creeping stems which run over the surface; also spreads by seed
Creeping thistle *Cirsium arvense*	Perennial	Prickly leaves; very deep, brittle roots, fragments of which will regrow
Common dandelion *Taraxacum officinale*	Perennial	Rosette-leaved with thick tap roots, fragments of which will regrow; also spreads by seed
Dock genus *Rumex*	Perennial	Rosette-leaved with thick tap roots; seeds prolifically
Fat hen *Chenopodium album*	Annual	Tall and bushy; seeds prolifically
Ground elder *Aegopodium podagraria*	Perennial	Low growing; spreads by invasive underground stems, fragments of which will regrow
Groundsel *Senecio vulgaris*	Annual	Short and bushy; seeds almost all year round
Hairy bittercress *Cardamine hirsuta*	Annual	Rosette-leaved; seeds prolifically however small the plant
Hedge bindweed *Calystegia sepium*	Perennial	Twines up plant stems, hedges, and other supports; has deep, invasive, underground stems
Horsetail *Equisetum arvense*	Perennial	Erect, spiky; deep, underground stems, fragments of which will regrow
Oxalis (genus *Oxalis*)	Perennial	Low-growing; delicate foliage; has small bulbils which easily break off and spread
Stinging **nettle** *Urtica dioica*	Perennial	Bushy foliage; tough, spreading, roots; also spreads by seed

Method of control	Comments
Hoeing	Not easily killed by **flameweeding**
Hoeing or **digging** it in	Acts like a **green manure**, but catch it before it seeds; the leaves are good in salads; **birds** love the seeds
Apply a **mulch** or fork regularly to remove the roots	The roots have herbal uses
Hoeing or forking, especially before creeping stems make new roots	Common in damp soils, where weeding is more difficult
Mulching over several growing seasons, or forking to remove roots	
Digging up roots or mulching	The leaves are good in salads; **bees** and other insects love the flowers, which are used for making wine
Digging up roots or mulching	If the top 15cm (6in) of a root is removed, it will not regrow
Hoeing or hand **weeding**, or mulching when young	The cooked leaves are edible
Mulching, over one or two growing seasons, or persistent hoeing or forking to remove roots	
Hoeing or hand weeding	Birds love the seeds
Hoeing or hand weeding	Often brought in by container-grown plants; the leaves are good in salads
As for creeping thistle	Almost impossible to eradicate from among established plants once entangled in their roots
As for creeping thistle	
Mulching over several growing seasons, or digging up of isolated plants with surrounding soil	Avoid other methods, which tend to spread the bulbils
Mulching or regular forking to remove roots	See main entry

Weevils small beetles, some species of which are vegetable-eating, such as the bean and the **vine weevil**.

White currants see **Bush fruit**.

Whitefly, brassica tiny white flies (with similar habits to glasshouse **whitefly**), which are **pests** of **brassica** plants. They form sooty moulds on plants, but these do not necessarily make the plants less edible, and seldom weaken them. Pick off badly infested leaves. To reduce future attacks, pull up plant stumps after harvest, and remove overwintered brassicas before putting out new plants in spring. As a last resort, spray with **insecticidal soap**.

Whitefly, glasshouse tiny, white, sap-feeding flies, which are serious **pests** in **greenhouses**, affecting many food crops and ornamental plants. They feed on the underside of leaves, and fly up when disturbed. Sooty moulds form on the "honeydew" which the flies excrete. This can make plants look unsightly, and bad attacks can weaken them.

Examine plants regularly so that you can act at the first sign of the pest. Spray local infestations with **insecticidal soap**. You can prevent the pest from reaching damaging levels by introducing a **biological control** - the **parasitic wasp** *Encarsia formosa*. You can also try sucking the whitefly up with a vacuum cleaner after first disturbing the plant's leaves to make the pest fly.

White rot a serious **disease** of **onions** and **garlic**, which also affects **leeks**, **shallots**, and chives. It causes leaves to turn yellow and die back, and a fluffy, white mould, containing black pinheads, to develop around the roots. To prevent this disease, use as long a crop **rotation** as possible. Do not bring in plants of the onion family which may carry the infection, since once the **soil** is contaminated, it is almost impossible to eradicate the disease. Remove and destroy isolated, affected plants, together with several spadesful of the surrounding soil, to prevent the disease spreading.

Wildflower meadow a traditional meadow containing a wide variety of wild grass and flower species, which will attract far more wildlife than ordinary grassland and also provide nutrient-rich **hay** for livestock and for use as a **mulch**. You can create a wildflower meadow as part of a nature garden

(see pp. 144-5). Ideally, replace the top **soil** with poor soil
and sow a mixture of native wildflower and meadow grass
seeds (see Useful Addresses, pp. 190-1). Alternatively,
reduce **soil fertility** by removing mowings over several
years. Raise wildflowers in pots before planting out. Opt
for spring flowers and mow from July onward, or grow
summer flowers and mow up until June and again from
late September. Rake off any **hay** to keep fertility low.

Wildflowers see **Native plants**.

Wildlife gardening see **Nature gardening**.

Willows a broad variety of plants in the genus *Salix*, ranging from tiny mountainside or heath plants to the weeping
willow **tree**. Many willows are fast growing and will take
readily from **cuttings**; the resultant "whips", once planted
out, will reach a fair height in just a few years. These are
quick to form a **windbreak** but need plenty of moisture and
have invasive roots and therefore are really only suitable
for a large garden. However, there are some less vigorous
species. **Coppicing** larger trees will provide firewood.

Wildflowers
**Wildlife
gardening**
Willows
Windbreak

Windbreak any structure that serves to shelter your garden
from the wind. It may consist of a **hedge**, **wall**, **fencing**, or
plastic windbreak material. Windbreaks will not only
reduce direct damage to plants, but will help **pollination**
and increase the yields of many **fruit** and **vegetable** crops.

   The best windbreaks are those that are 50% holes, since
they slow down the wind but still allow a free flow of air.
You can make them from slatted fencing, windbreak **netting**, and some hedges. Avoid solid windbreaks which can
create damaging eddies in their lee when the wind goes
up and over them. They can also produce stagnant conditions which encourage fungal **diseases**, and can trap cold
air and cause a **frost** pocket.

   A windbreak provides shelter over a distance about 10
times its height. Thus, the taller it is, the more of the garden it will cover, although you also have to consider the
shading that such barriers create. Hedges will compete
with neighbouring plants for water and **nutrients**, but on
balance are still probably the best type of windbreak.
From an ecological point of view, they are superior to
plastic or treated **timber**.

Wind generation the use of wind as a source of **energy**. You can adapt the traditional windmill design to pump water, in which case it is called a wind pump, or to drive a generator for electricity, in which case it is known as an aero-generator. In the garden, you could use wind generation to charge a battery for lighting a shed, or to power an **electric fence**. You can make a battery charger very simply by adapting an old bicycle wheel.

Window gardening for the urban dweller, frequently the only form of gardening possible. You can grow any number of house plants indoors, but if you have a sun-facing window sill and/or ledge you can experiment with a range of food crops. If you have limited space it is probably worth concentrating on those you will have difficulty in buying fresh, such as **herbs**, particularly tender ones, and some of the **vegetables** which will not grow outside in Britain. **Sprouting** beans, grains, and seeds is a good way of getting fresh green produce in the winter.

Winter moth a brown moth, whose "looper" caterpillars damage **apples**, **pears**, **plums**, and some ornamental plants. They feed on buds, blossom, and young leaves, and can affect yields and weaken plants. In midsummer, they drop to the soil to pupate, and the adults emerge between October and April. Prevent attacks by putting **greasebands** on tree trunks and stakes to catch the wingless female moths climbing up to lay their eggs. Have them in place from the end of September up until the end of April. In summer, **handpick** caterpillars by hand. Only as a last resort, spray fruit trees with the **natural insecticide**, **derris**, as the flower buds begin to burst.

Wireworms the larvae of various species of click beetle (see p. 17). They are thin, yellowy brown, up to 2.5cm (1in) long, and live in the **soil**, feeding on the roots, corms, tubers, and stems of many **vegetables** and ornamental plants. Wireworms can also attack **strawberries**. The click beetles lay their eggs in grassland and weedy ground, so wireworms are mainly a problem in plots recently brought under cultivation, although they can carry on feeding for up to five years before pupating. Affected seedlings wilt and die, and mature plants loose their vigour. **Carrots** and **potatoes** are left with small holes.

Cultivate infested land regularly to expose the larvae, and to keep it **weed** free. Over small areas, you can catch wireworms by using pieces of potato or carrot, spiked on sticks, as bait and burying them in the ground. Replace these regularly. Harvest potatoes in early September to minimise damage, since the larvae feed mainly from March to May, and in September and October.

Wood see **Timber, sustainable**.

Wood ash a source of **potassium** which you can add to the **compost heap**, although it should not make up more than about 10% of the total. You can also try laying a trail of ash around seedlings as a **slug barrier**, although this will only work, if at all, while the ash remains dry. Do not apply wood ash directly to the **soil** since it dissolves too readily. And, unless you are adding it immediately to the compost heap, you will need to store it under cover.

Woodchips a useful **weed**-suppressing **mulch**, which breaks down gradually, adding **organic matter** to the soil. Avoid chips treated with **wood preservative** since these can remain toxic for years. If the woodchips are the result of your own prunings, leave them to weather before use.

Woodlice in the garden, generally harmless crustacean invertebrates which have eight armour-like segments on their back. Woodlice live in damp places, under rocks and wood, and feed on rotted plant material. They occasionally eat germinating seeds and young plants, particularly if they find their way into a **greenhouse**. To discourage them, move away objects that provide moist hiding places, such as old seed trays, slates, and plant debris.

Wood preservatives any **pesticide** used to protect wood from insect and fungal attack. Much outdoor **timber** is treated with wood preservatives, such as **creosote**, while timber in barns and sheds sometimes receives applications of **gamma HCH** and **pentachlorphenol**. All of these pose health and environmental hazards. See **Timber treatment** for safer, alternative methods of treating wood.

Woolly aphid a small, brown insect covered in a white, fluffy wax. It is a common **pest** of **apples**, but also affects

crab apples, **cotoneaster**, **hawthorn**, **pyracantha**, and some other plants. Woolly aphids cause irregular swellings, or galls, on twigs and branches, which can disfigure young trees. On mature trees, serious damage only occurs if the swellings crack open and allow **disease** organisms to enter. On affected plants, scrape off the fluffy colonies as soon as they appear. Prune out and burn badly galled branches. One small **parasitic wasp** is a **natural predator** of woolly aphids, so avoid spraying except as a last resort. If you have to spray, try regular applications of **insecticidal soap**.

Wormbin
Wormcasts
Worm compost
Worms

Wormbin a container within which **brandling worms** feed on decaying organic material to provide useful **compost**. The worms like to be fed little and often, so a wormbin is an ideal way of **recycling** daily **kitchen waste**. You can make one yourself from, for example, a wooden box or a plastic dustbin (see p. 50). Put the worms on to a suitably moist bedding, such as **leafmould**, and add scraps or garden waste for them to feed on. The worms work best between 50°F (10°C) and 68°F (20°C). Under these conditions you should have usable **worm compost** after six months.

Wormcasts the pellets of soil deposited by **earthworms**, most familiar as the coils which appear on the surface of a **lawn**. They are rich in **minerals** and **organic matter**, and have a very stable structure, remaining crumbly, even when wet or trampled upon. They are a welcome sign of worm activity. On a lawn, brush them over the surface with a stiff broom before mowing, if necessary. You can also buy packets of wormcasts, which are the result of very well-worked **worm compost** and have similar uses.

Worm compost a valuable product, resulting from the activity of **brandling worms** in a **wormbin**, which is high in **nutrients** with a very stable structure. It is most useful for top dressing plants in containers or as an ingredient of **seed** and **potting composts**. However, some worm compost is made at intensive **rabbit** farms, where the worms break down droppings from rabbits kept above them in tiny cages. For this reason, you may want to check the source of worm compost before purchasing it.

Worms see **Brandling worms** and **Earthworms**.

Yarrow a hardy perennial, *Achillea millefolium*, which is a **weed** of **lawns** and waste ground, although cultivated **varieties** are useful **attractant plants**, especially for **hoverflies** and **lacewings**. They are also loved by **bees**. Yarrow will grow easily on any well-drained, sunny site.

Zineb a widely used **fungicide**, currently under suspicion of having long-term health effects. It is an eye, skin, and respiratory system **irritant** and a suspect **carcinogen** and **mutagen**. Along with **maneb** and **mancozeb**, it is being investigated by the US Environmental Protection Agency because of the possible health risks associated with its **residues** in food: these can contain **ethylene thiourea**. Zineb has moderate **persistence** and **harvest intervals** ranging from two days to one month. Try **cultural control** instead.

Organizations

Organic Growing Associations

Biodynamic Agricultural
Association (BDAA)
Woodman Lane
Clent
Stourbridge
DY9 9PX
0562 884933

British Organic Farmers/
The Organic Growers
Association (BOF/OGA)
86 Colston Street
Bristol BS1 5BB
0272 299666/299800

Centre for Alternative
Technology (CAT)
Llwyngwern Quarry
Machynlleth
Powys SY20 9AZ
0654 702400

Elm Farm Research Centre
(EFRC)
Hamstead Marshall
Newbury
Berks RG15 0HR
0488 58298
*Soil-testing service for
organic growers*

Henry Doubleday Research
Association (HDRA)
Ryton Gardens
Ryton-on-Dunsmore
Coventry CV8 3LG
0203 303517

The Permaculture
Association
Old Cuming Farm
Buckfastleigh
Devon TQ11 0LP
0364 43988

The Soil Association (SA)
86 Colston Street
Bristol BS1 5BB
0272 290661

Working Weekends on
Organic Farms (WWOOF)
19 Bradford Road
Lewes
Sussex BN7 1RB
0273 476286

Conservation Societies

The Bat Conservation Trust
c/o The Conservation
Foundation
1 Kensington Gore
London SW7 2AR

British Beekeepers
Association
National Agricultural Centre
Stoneleigh
Kenilworth
Warwicks CV8 2LZ
0203 696679

British Butterfly
Conservation Society
PO Box 222
Dedham
Colchester
Essex
0509 412870

British Hedgehog
Preservation Society
Knowbury House
Knowbury
Ludlow
Shropshire SY8 3JT

English Nature (EN)
Northminster House
Northminster Road
Peterborough
Cambs PE1 1UA
0733 340345

equivalent bodies
performing similar functions
to the EN in Scotland,
Wales, and Northern
Ireland are:

- The Nature Conservancy
  Council for Scotland
  12 Hope Terrace
  Edinburgh EH9 2AS
  031 447 4784

- The Countryside Council
  for Wales
  Plas Penrhos
  Bangor
  Gwynned LL57 2LQ
  0248 370444

- The Department of the
  Environment
  Calvert House

Castle Place
Belfast BT1 1FA
0232 230 560

The Marine Conservation
Society
9 Gloucester Road
Herefordshire HR9 5BU
0989 66017

Men of the Trees
Turners Hill Road
Crawley Down
Crawley
West Sussex RH10 4HL
0342 712536

National Council for the
Conservation of Plants and
Gardens (NCCPG)
The Pines
Wisley Gardens
Woking
Surrey GU23 6QB
0483 211465

Royal Society for the
Protection of Birds (RSPB)
The Lodge
Sandy
Beds SG19 2DL
0767 80551

RSNC Wildlife Trust
Partnership
The Green
Witham Park
Lincoln LN5 7JR
0522 544400

Wild Flower Society
68 Outwoods Road
Loughborough
Leics LE11 3LY
0509 215598

Wildlife Trust
contact the RSNC Wildlife
Trust Partnership (see
above) to obtain the
address of your local
Wildlife Trust

Woodland Trust
Autumn Park
Dysart Road
Grantham
Lincs NG31 6LL
0476 74297

Environmental Organizations

Friends of the Earth (FOE)
26-28 Underwood Street
London N1 7JQ
071 490 1555

Greenpeace
Canonbury Villas
London N1 2PN
071 354 5100

The International Pesticides
Action Network
c/o The Pesticide Trust
23 Beehive Place
London SW9 7QR
071 274 8895

London Ecology Centre
45 Shelton Street
London WC2H 9HJ
071 379 4324

National Society for Clean
Air and Protection of the
Environment
136 North Street
Brighton BN1 1RG
0273 26313

Suppliers

The following organizations
all have a mail-order
service.

Chase Organics (GB) Ltd
Coombelands Lane
Addlestone
Weighbridge
Surrey KT15 1HY
0932 858511
*Wide range of organic
gardening materials*

John Chambers
15 Westleigh Road
Barton Seagrave
Kettering
Northants NN15 5AJ
0933 652562
*Seeds of native wild
flowers and mixes; grasses;
herbs; and green manure
crops*

HDRA (Sales) Limited
Ryton Gardens
Ryton-on-Dunsmore
Coventry CV8 3LG
0203 303517
*Full range of organic
gardening materials,
including: untreated seeds;
biological controls; traps,
barriers, and fleeces; and
compost bins*

Seed Savers Exchange
Rural Route 3
Box 239
Decorah
Iowa 52101
*Yearly publication through
which members can offer
and track down unique
vegetable varieties*

Suffolk Herbs Ltd
Sawyers Farm
Little Cornards
Sudbury
Suffolk CO10 0NY
0787 227247
*Seeds of herbs, wild
flowers, vegetables, and
traditional cottage-garden
plants*

Authors' acknowledgements

The authors would like to
thank Dr Andrew Watterson
of Southampton University
and Dr Jeremy Light of the
Centre of Alternative
Technology in Wales for
their careful reading of the
text, and Eliot Coleman for
his contribution to the US
edition of the book. Thanks
are also due to Joss
Pearson at Gaia Books for
initiating the project; to
Gian Douglas Home and
Fiona Trent for subjecting
the text to searching
scrutiny; and to Marnie
Searchwell for design
expertise.

Publisher's acknowledgements

Gaia Books extends thanks
to the following for their
help in producing this book:
Dr Jeremy Light, Dr Andrew
Watterson, and Eliot
Coleman; Juliet Bailey and
Isabelle Gore for editorial
assistance; Babz Scott for
her lively illustrations; Sara
Mathews for design liaison;
Phil Gamble for design
assistance; Susan Walby
and Alison Jones for
production; Libby Hoseason
for coordination; and
Lesley Gilbert for text
management.

NEW FROM GAIA BOOKS

Gaia's new **Eco A-Z Series**, featuring practical reference guides for today's health- and planet-conscious readers.

Published simultaneously with **G is for ecoGarden**:

H is for ecoHome

An A-Z Guide to a Healthy, Planet-Friendly Household by Anna Kruger

This concise directory of common household chemicals and indoor pollutants tells you everything you need to know about personal and environmental safety in the home. It is a realistic guide to the affordable and ecologically sound alternatives available.

Anna Kruger is an experienced writer and environmental researcher. She has acted as consultant to major UK publishers for their MIND/ BODY/SPIRIT lists, and is currently writing an illustrated herbal.

ISBN 1 85675 030 2

To be published in Spring 1992

R is for Reuse, Repair, Recycle

by Jan McHarry

After decades of profligate use of the Earth's resources, the ideas of reusing and recycling are catching on. People everywhere are now beginning to realize that all "waste" is potential wealth. And, most importantly, the actions of every one of us do count. In the home or at work, the practical, good-sense information contained in **R is for Reuse, Repair, Recycle** will become a natural part of our everyday lives. Indeed, it may even lead to a whole new lifestyle: revolutionizing our attitudes to shopping, sharing goods, and learning new skills.

Jan McHarry was until recently Chief Information Officer of Friends of the Earth, and was FOE's representative on many non-governmental committees and organizations. Jan's background makes her a natural communicator, and her close connection with the many groups campaigning on environmental issues has given her access to the most up-to-date research from around the world.

ISBN 1 85675 045 0